Perceiving Syllables and Contrasts

KLEAR-RILI Studies in Korean Language and Linguistics

THE KOREAN LANGUAGE EDUCATION AND RESEARCH CENTER &
THE RESEARCH INSTITUTE OF LANGUAGE AND INFORMATION

PERCEIVING SYLLABLES AND CONTRASTS

Second Language Learning Perspectives

Byung-jin Lim

KOREA
UNIVERSITY
PRESS
고려대학교
출판문화원

Korea University Press
82-2-3290-4234 (Tel.) 82-2-923-6311 (Fax)
http://www.kupress.com kupress@korea.ac.kr
145, Anam-Ro, Seongbuk-Gu, Seoul, 02841 Korea

Published August 2015

ISBN 978-89-7641-884-5 93710

KRW 23,000

PRINTED IN REPUBLIC OF KOREA

EDITORIAL STATEMENT

The Korean Language Education and Research Center, Inc. (KLEAR) in Honolulu, Hawai'i, and the Research Institute of Language Information (RILI) at Korea University initiated the KLEAR-RILI Studies series in Korean Language and Linguistics in 2013 in order to promote studies on the Korean language worldwide. This multi-volume series is aimed at publishing, through the Korea University Press, scholarly manuscripts, written mainly in English, which deal with the linguistic structure, change and variation, language use, teaching, and learning of the Korean language.

It is well known that a large number of important studies conducted in overseas institutions of higher education on a variety of aspects of Korean have remained unpublished, being unable to find an appropriate international publisher for the obvious reason that an in-depth study on a specific area or issue in Korean generally fails to attract wide international readership. Under these circumstances, our goal is to cover a broad spectrum of research areas, capture state-of-the-art studies on Korean language and linguistics, and expeditiously bring significant research findings to light.

The KLEAR-RILI series accommodates not only monographs, anthologies, and edited books, but also, from 2015, revised versions of outstanding doctoral dissertations that are written in English. The series accommodates theoretical, descriptive, and applied studies on the one hand and both formal and functional approaches on the other.

One cataclysmic change in the history of the teaching of Korean as a foreign language is the unprecedentedly rapid growth of student enrollments in Korean language classes around the globe during the past fifteen years or so. In the United States, Korean has shown the largest increase in student enrollment among all modern foreign languages. This dramatic increase in enrollments in Korean calls for extensive pedagogical research in order to better serve the diverse needs of the ever-increasing population of learners of Korean. The KLEAR-RILI series is prepared to publish such pedagogical works, as well.

Ho-min Sohn
KLEAR President &
Professor of Korean Language and Linguistics
University of Hawai'i at Mānoa

Seok-Hoon You
RILI and the Korea University Press Director &
Professor of Linguistics
Korea University

Acknowledgements

The journey of writing this book began with a blessing because I have received unimaginable support and encouragement from many wonderful people.

I am extremely grateful to Professor Ken de Jong who was my advisor, teacher, and big brother during the entire process of writing this book. Without his endless encouragement and confidence in me, this book would never have become a reality. His insightful comments and inspiring ideas were always amazing and stimulating.

Special thanks go to Professors Stuart Davis, Bob Port, and Diane Kewley-Port at Indiana University. I benefited tremendously from their deep knowledge of phonology, phonetics, and speech sciences for this book project.

I would also like to express my deepest thanks to my former professors at Korea University, Kee-Ho Kim, Yong-Jae Lee, and Kyung-Ja Park, for constant encouragement and unending attention to their former student.

I was privileged to work with caring and inspiring colleagues at the University of Wisconsin-Madison. Especially, I am grateful to Naomi Geyer, Junko Mori, and Naomi McGloin who were always available to share their experiences and point me in the right direction whenever I felt lost. In addition, my very special thanks go to Nicole Huang and Monika Chavez, my mentors and role models, who never failed to find time to guide me and cheer me up.

I would like to express my sincere gratitude to Professor Seok-Hoon You and his staff of the Korea University Press for providing this opportunity to publish my research and for their helpful advice in the preparation of the manuscript. I am also very grateful to Karen Best for her editorial work.

My heartfelt thanks go to my best friends, Jeff Kloko and Nancy Jo Grochowski, for their unfailing support and endless love, which has enabled me to complete the process of writing this book.

Above all, I owe a true debt of gratitude to my parents, Kil-Yong Lim and Insoon Ko, my two brothers, Moo-hwee Lim and Jee-joon Lim, and my sister, Jiyoung Lim, for their incredible support and love throughout the journey.

I dedicate this book to my mom who showed great courage in the face of cancer and ultimately won that battle – through it all she showed me that "Life is good."

THANK YOU ALL!

Contents

List of Tables

List of Figures

CHAPTER 1

INTRODUCTION

Focus of Research

Decoding speech requires people to map onto stored network of information, and thus they are able to construct interpretations of the speakers' intentions. This book investigates the process of **segmentation (or syllabification[1]),** through which a continuous speech stream in a language is broken into meaningful units such that the information carried in spoken utterances or represented in orthography is relayed to language users.

The book will provide cross-linguistic comparison of the process of segmentation by focusing on whether and how a certain segmentation strategy observed in a first language (L1) is maintained when the speaker is parsing a typologically different language (L2). As linguists attempt to understand how different components of speech comprehension processes are influenced by language-specific and/or language-general phonological knowledge, it is essential that cross-linguistic perspectives are part of the literature. The research presented here is particularly interested in looking at cross-linguistic variations of EFL/ESL (English as a Foreign/Second Language[2]) learners' strategies from various angles: *perception, production,* and *orthography*. Therefore, a part of this book

---

1 I will use segmentation and syllabification interchangeably throughout the book.

2 Second vs. foreign language learning (Oxford, 1996)

a) **Second language learning**: occurs in contexts in which the language is readily available in the community and students have many opportunities to experience it.

b) **Foreign language learning**: occurs when the language is not commonly used in the community and there is little opportunity to experience the language outside of the classroom.

will emphasize whether a certain segmentation strategy observed in a language is retained when a speaker of a particular language, *in this case Korean*, parses a typologically different language, *in this case English*.

In addition, the book further asks whether the mechanism for and representation of decoding speech chains develop or change as a result of exposure to new languages. Another question that needs to be addressed throughout the book concerns the effects of segmentation units of the native language (L1) on target language (L2) learning. Finally, I attempt to determine how the written form of a language relates not just to pronunciation, but also to other levels of linguistic knowledge, in particular looking closely at Korean orthographic representations of English words. Korean is relatively transparent in terms of mapping sounds onto letters, and it has a fairly simple syllable structure.[3] Therefore, Korean is a good testing ground for investigating how a typologically different language, *here English*, whose syllabification of medial clusters is not immediately clear, is perceived, parsed, and thus represented in a writing system which has clear syllable divisions. Along this line, the current book will develop an understanding of how Korean-speaking learners' knowledge of orthographies (L1 and L2) affects perception of syllables and voicing contrasts in the speech production of English.

Segmentation

Previous studies have suggested that there are rhythmic cues for segmentation which differ by language: Syllable-based segmentation in French (Mehler, Dommergues, Frauenfelder, & Segui, 1981; Cutler, Mehler, Norris, & Segui, 1986), mora-based segmentation in Japanese (Otake, Hatano, Cutler, & Mehler,1993), and strong-syllable-based

---

3 Syllable structure determines which sequences of consonants and vowels are allowed in a language: For example, if a language A has only CV syllables, it will have different sequences of consonant and vowel than a language B which has CV, CVC, and CCCVCCC syllables.

segmentation in English (Cutler & Norris, 1988) and Dutch (Quené & Koster, 1998).

In a word-recognition experiment in French, Mehler et al. (1981) found that the syllable plays an important role in the recognition of French. They showed that French speakers responded faster when the target sequence (either CV or CVC syllabic structure) corresponded exactly to the initial syllable of the target-bearing word than when the target sequence constituted more or less than the initial syllable. For example, responses to *ba-* were faster in 'balance' than in 'balcon,' while responses to *bal-* were faster in 'balcon' than in 'balance'. This syllable-based segmentation by the French is also found when using English (Norris & Segui, 1986).

On the other hand, English speakers did not show the same pattern as the French did (Cutler et al., 1986): English listeners' response time to *ba-* and *bal-* targets was not significantly different in either 'balance' or 'balcony' in the exactly same experimental design used in Mehler et al. (1981). For the English segmentation, Cutler and Norris (1988) proposed that the English segmentation procedure is strong-syllable-based. Their proposal is based on a hypothcsis, *Strong Syllable Segmentation Hypothesis*, which proposes that segmentation for lexical access occurs at strong syllables. In a word-detection experiment in which real words were embedded in nonsense words they found that English speakers detected the embedded real word *mint* faster in 'mintesh' than in 'mintayve'. In 'mintayve,' the second syllable *tayve* is strong. According to the Strong Syllable Segmentation Hypothesis, segmentation and lexical access initiate at 'tayve,' which interferes with the detection of 'mint' because part of the word 'mint' belongs to both syllables. Thus, "successful detection of 'mint' requires assembly of material across a point at which the signal has been segmented" (Cutler & Norris, 1988, p. 114). When the second syllable is weak as in 'mintesh', however, there is no segmentation, and thus, no interference. Therefore, the 'mint' in *mintesh* is detected faster than in *mintayve*. These different segmentation patterns based on language-specific rhythmic cues may account for why the rhythm of English phrases may be distorted when produced by non-native learners, whose native segmentation cues are different from those of English.

It is not an easy task to parse a segment that seems to belong to two syllables simultaneously. In general, the segmentation process captures this segment, and aligns it either as the coda of one syllable or the onset of the next/following syllable. In some cases, though, the segment in question is assigned to both syllables, in which case it is called an *ambisyllabic* segment. My main interest is focused on this latter case, **ambisyllabicity**. I am in particular interested in the cross-linguistic variation in English as second/foreign language (ESL/EFL) learners' segmentation of intervocalic consonants; therefore, I also consider some important properties of a learner's interlanguage[4] within the context of the Interlanguage Hypothesis (Selinker, 1972) and the Markedness Differential Hypothesis (Eckman, 1977, 1981a, 1981b). In so doing, I investigate syllabification patterns of English intervocalic consonants, employing Korean-speaking learners of English in a wide variety of linguistic environments while using syllable-detection and syllable-reversal tasks (cf. Treiman & Danis, 1988). I further discuss pedagogical implications of the syllabification of ambisyllabic consonants, following Trammell (1999) who noted that: "attention to ambisyllabic articulations will produce more native-like allophones and syllabification, which in turn will lead to a better approximation of English stress patterns and, hence, authentic English phrasal rhythm"(p. 325).

4 The term 'interlanguage' was proposed by Selinker (1969) and then elaborated in Selinker (1972) to account for the unique utterances of second language learners. "Selinker postulates the existence of a system somewhere between the native language and the language to be learned. This system he termed 'interlanguage', defining it as a 'separate linguistic system based on observable output which results from a learner's attempted production of a target language norm', where the target language is defined as 'one norm of one dialect'."(Thiede, 1997)

Ambisyllabicity

In the following sections, I briefly survey previous approaches to syllabification of intervocalic consonants mainly in English from various perspectives: 1) linguistic accounts, 2) psycholinguistic accounts and, 3) computational accounts.

Linguistic Accounts: Syllabification of Ambisyllabicity

Ambisyllabicity is traditionally defined as the double-affiliation of an intervocalic consonant to both the preceding and following syllables.[5] The existence of ambisyllabicity supports Kahn's (1976) autosegmental treatment of the syllable: Kahn's proposal makes it possible for a consonant to become ambisyllabic by having the consonant linking two syllable unless it violates the line-crossing constraint (Goldsmith, 1976). The syllabification of ambisyllabic consonants in English is affected by the identify of the vowel (Pulgram, 1970), speech rates (Kahn, 1976), and representations (Selkirk, 1982). Table 1.1 shows some examples of English syllabification.

Table 1.1. English syllabification of intervocalic consonants

Pulgram (1970)	demon → de-mon	lemon → lem-on
Kahn (1976)	demote → de-mote (slow) demote → de-mote (normal/fast)	lemon → le-mon (slow) lemon → lem-mon (normal/fast)
Selkirk (1982)	demote → de-mote (Deep-level) demote → de-mote (Surface-level)	lemon → le-mon (Deep-level) lemon → lem-on (Surface-level)

According to Pulgram (1970), the nature of the first vowel determines

5 "Ambisyllabicity, or partial resyllabification, traditionally describes the joint affiliation of an intervocalic consonant with two flanking vocalic peaks (with or without intervening word or other boundaries). A reformulation of ambisyllabicity in terms of Articulatory Phonology (AP) would therefore state that certain intervocalic gestures are crucially phased to both the preceding and the following vowel gestures." (Gick, 2003, p. 226)

syllabification of the intervocalic consonants. That is, if the first vowel can end a word, the intervocalic consonant belongs to the second syllable. On the other hand, if the first vowel is not allowed in the word-final position, the intervocalic consonant belongs to the first syllable. In Kahn's (1976) theory of syllabification in English, syllabification is also sensitive to speech rate: In slow speech, the onsets of all syllables take consonants as long as possible unless the consonant clusters are illegal for phonotactics. However, in normal and fast speech, intervocalic consonants are assigned to the second syllable (e.g., de-mote) or attached to both preceding and following syllables, *ambisyllabic*, as shown in the example of 'lemon' (lem-mon) above. Selkirk (1982) posits that words are syllabified on two levels: 1) an underlying or deep level and 2) a surface or phonetic level.

Psycholinguistic Accounts: Paralinguistic Syllabification Studies

To incorporate the linguistic work into the psychological work on syllabification, Treiman and Danis (1988) used two syllable-reversal tasks to examine the relationship of syllabification between oral and written forms in English. Specifically, they examined the effects of stress-placement, the phonetic nature of intervocalic consonants, and spellings of the intervocalic consonants on syllabification in English.

In Experiment 1 (Treiman & Danis, 1988), English-speaking participants were asked to produce bisyllabic words starting from the second syllable for the oral task (e.g., snowman → man-snow/catfood → food-cat). For the written task, each stimulus was typed in two ways with a slash before or after the intervocalic letters (e.g., pro/per and prop/er; co/mmand and comm/and). The participants were asked to choose the preferred syllabification in each pair. The results of Experiment 1 show the effects of stress and spelling on syllabification. In the oral task, when the second syllable was stressed, participants placed the consonant in the second syllable significantly more often than they placed it in the first syllable; whereas when the first syllable was stressed, participants showed no reliable preference for placing the consonant in the first or second syllable. The participants more often placed the consonant in both syllables when the first syllable was stressed than when the second syllable was stressed. They also show that English-speaking participants are more likely to place the critical consonant sound in both syllables when it is spelled with a double letter than with a single letter. The results of the written task in Experiment 1 show that, as in the oral task, the proportion of the first syllable responses was higher when the first syllable was stressed than when the second syllable was stressed. In addition, participants were more likely to place the critical consonant in the first syllable when it was spelled with two letters than when it was spelled with one letter.

In Experiment 2, Treiman and Danis (1988) used a similar procedure as in Experiment 1, but they varied the phonetic category of the intervocalic consonants (i.e., liquid, nasal, or obstruent). Results show that participants were more likely to place an intervocalic liquid or nasal in both syllables than an intervocalic obstruent in an oral task. On the other hand, participants made more first syllable attachments for liquids and nasals than for obstruents in a written task.

Regarding the relationship between spoken and written forms of a language, Treiman and Danis's (1988) results agree with previous studies (Ehri & Wilce, 1986; Jakimik, Cole, & Rudnicky, 1985; Seidenberg & Tanenhaus, 1979) in that "even in an oral task, people's responses may be affected by how they spell the words" (p. 89).

Computational Accounts: Segmentation Cues

Computational approaches use various cues for segmentation: Rhythmic, allophonic and phonotactic cues. Brent (1999, p.3) eloquently summarizes recent proposals of computational accounts on speech segmentation cues as follows:

> First, some languages provide what Cutler and colleagues have called rhythmic cues (Mehler et al., 1981; Cutler et al, 1986; Otake et al., 1993; Cutler & Norris, 1988; Quené & Koster, 1998). For example, most

> stressed syllables in English are word-initial (Cutler & Carter, 1987), and adult speakers of English find it more natural to segment connected speech in such a way that stressed syllables occur at the beginning of words (Cutler & Norris, 1988; Cutler & Butterfield, 1992). Language learners following such a strategy might eliminate candidate words containing non-initial stressed syllable, thereby reducing the number of candidates. Second, children might use allophonic variation cues — the fact that some speech sounds are pronounced differently when they occur word-finally as opposed to word-initially (Church, 1987; Gow & Gordon, 1995). A third type of cue derives from the phonotactic properties of a language. While rhythmic cues have been minor players in computational models of language learning and allophonic cues have not appeared at all, phonotactic cues in various forms have featured prominently in several models (Aslin, Woodward, LaMendola, & Bever, 1996; Christiansen, Allen, & Seidenberg, 1998).

So far I have shown various perspectives on the syllabification of intervocalic consonants in English. As previously mentioned, I am particularly interested in Korean EFL/ESL (English as a foreign/second language) learners' syllabification of intervocalic consonants (i.e., V<u>C</u>V) in English. Before I move on to the syllabification patterns of intervocalic English consonants by Korean-speaking learners of English, I begin by presenting the reader with an overview of the **Korean** language in the following sections.

Korean

Why Korean?

A main focus of this book is the comparison of Korean with English. The reasons that Korean was chosen for the current study are three-fold. First, Korean is transparent in terms of mapping sounds onto letters such that the relationship between spoken and written representations of speech is relatively straightforward. Second, the Korean orthographic representation is visually syllable-based in that each syllable should be expressed within a virtual syllabic block. That is, the orthography reveals clear syllable divisions within words. Third, Korean syllable structure is simpler than English, and it does not allow consonant clusters either syllable-initially or syllable-finally. Thus, the syllable starts and ends with only a singleton on the phonetic level. Since the syllabification of medial clusters in English words is not immediately clear, this simple structure in Korean is a good testing ground for investigating how a typologically different language, *English*, is perceived, parsed, and thus represented in a writing system, *Korean*, where clear syllable divisions are shown. Therefore, Korean orthographic representations of English words are expected to show clear syllable divisions of the intervocalic consonants such as *hammer, pony,* and *Mississippi* which are controversial for English speakers to break up in terms of internal syllable boundaries.

Standard Korean and Standard English

The current study is based on research and experiments with the younger generation (i.e., college students) who live in the Seoul area. Speakers in this demographic generally speak what is called 'Standard Korean'. It is therefore important to attempt to define Standard Korean. To do this, I will begin by examining the literature about so-called 'Standard British English' or, *Received Pronunciation (RP) English*. The term 'received' in 'Received Pronunciation (RP) English' originally meant 'that which is generally accepted' or 'that accepted by the best society' ('Received Pronunciation English,' 2001, para 1). RP has for many years epitomized the "top end of the scale" of British English and it is what English people have traditionally meant when they have said someone has 'no accent'. It is often regarded as the "neutral" and "correct" accent. According to Wells (1982), it is also referred to under the terms "BBC English", "Public School English" or even "Standard English." RP is the accent that Americans would likely refer to as the typical British accent. It should also be noted that there is no single accent whose role and status in the United States corresponds to that of RP in England

(Wells, 1982). RP is not associated with any particular location within England. Because it is what might be thought of as an "educated accent," it appears characteristically in upper and upper middle class speakers, and is more likely sociologically defined rather than geographically defined. Wells (1982) points out how significantly speech differences are associated with social class differences in Britain by saying that "people are often able to make instant and unconscious judgments about a stranger's class affiliation on the basis of his or her accent".

Does anyone speak standard American English, then? There is no single dialect of American English that corresponds to a "standard" American English, although the popular belief is that such a dialect exists in the speech of those who use so-called "good" English (Preston, 1993, 1996). Wolfram, Adger, and Christian (1999, p. 14-15) point out that this belief is rooted in the social truth: "the speech of a certain social group of people does define what is considered standard in English. However, the norms for Standard English are not identical in all communities."

They also recognize two sets of norms, the *informal* standard and the *formal* standard:

> The norms of language usage that members of a community consider to be acceptable constitute the 'informal standard American English'. This set of norms relates to the way certain people actually speak and allows for variation between communities. 'Formal standard English', on the other hand, includes the norms prescribed in grammar books and is most typically reflected in the written language. (p. 15)

What about Standard Korean, then? According to the guidelines on the Pronunciation of Standard Korean by the Ministry of Education (1988), it is defined as "Modern Seoul Korean spoken by educated people". It is slightly modified from an original definition by '*chosuneu hakhoi*' (Korean language Study Circle) in 1933: 'Contemporary Seoul Korean spoken by middle-classed people'. Based on the above definition, Lee (1971) defined Standard Korean as "the speech of the middle class people native to Seoul" and Y-S. Hong (1991, p. 24-5) modified this into "the speech of the educated adults who were born and lived or have lived in Seoul from the age of five or so till the age of twenty or so."

It is even manifested in the guidelines that Standard Korean is an official speech in Korea with which anyone can use and, especially, people who are public figures must learn and use in their everyday lives. Thus, Standard Korean is defined chronologically, geographically, and sociologically: Contemporary Korean spoken in the area of Seoul, the capital of Korea, by the middle class educated people. However, this definition seems more or less abstract and arbitrary. It is quite true that the Seoul dialect is often identified with Standard Korean and both are usually used interchangeably (even in academia). Based on this definition, since that there are quite a few regional dialects within Seoul, there must be more than one possible Standard Korean available. In addition, the term 'educated people' is relative and not well-defined. It could refer to either anybody or nobody depending on how strictly the definition is applied. Similar to RP English in England, Standard Korean is closely associated with social class because the command of Standard Korean implicitly indicates that the person who utters the speech belongs to the ideal or even prestigious social classes.

My aim in this book is not to redefine 'Standard Korean' but rather to delineate which speakers the current study is dealing with, and clarify how they will be sampled. As shown in above definitions of Standard Korean, social class and geographical distribution seem to be determining factors for the Standard language. Furthermore, since the current study is primarily concerned with the speech of young people in the Seoul area, age should be another important factor. So, I will focus on the speech of members of the younger generation who were born in or after 1985 and have grown up in the Seoul area until the age of twenty (cf. Y-S. Hong, 1991). Geographical distribution in Korea is important in that it seems to be highly correlated with economic development and distribution of wealth, which results in higher education levels in the Seoul area.

Figure 1.1. Maps of Korean peninsula and Seoul
(from: www.lib.utexas.edu/maps/korea.html)

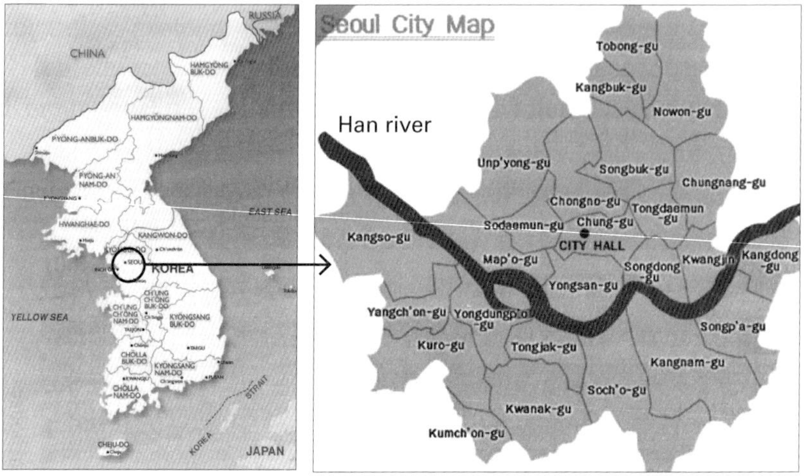

Syllable Structure in Korean

Korean has a simpler syllable structure than English[6]. It does not allow consonant clusters either syllable-initially or syllable-finally, and thus, it has the surface structure of (C)(G)V(C) on the phonetic level[7](cf. K.O. Kim & Shibatani, 1976). As indicated in the representation of the

6 A comparison between Korean and English in terms of syllable templates shows that English has typologically more complex syllable structures than Korean as shown below.

a) Complex onset "stream"

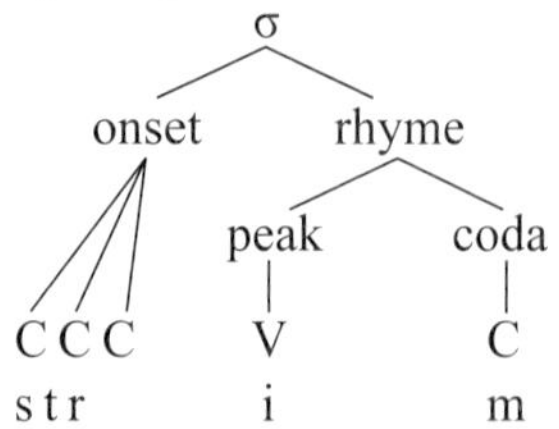

b. Complex coda "texts"

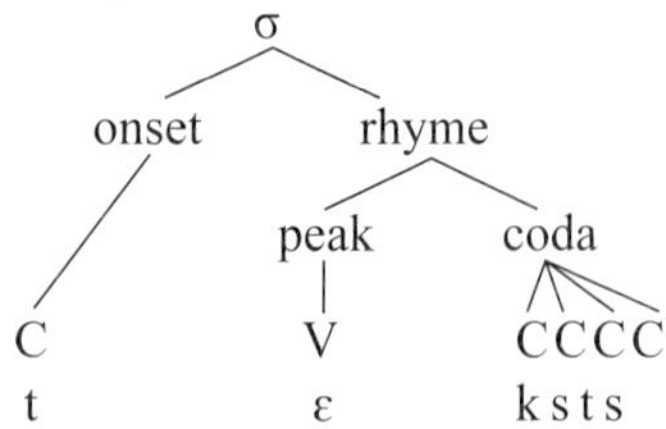

7 The constraints apply on the surface level which is distinguished from the underlying or deep level.

syllable structure, vowels are obligatory with optional accompaniment of preceding and/or following consonants. Examples (1) and (2) show exhaustive lists of the surface syllable structures in Korean.

(1) Open syllables

a. V	[i] (이)	'two'
b. CV	[sa] (사)	'four'
c. GV	[wa] (와)	'…and'
d. CGV	[kwa] (과)	'…and'

(2) Closed syllables

e. VC	[an] (안)	'inside'
f. CVC	[san] (산)	'mountain'
g. GVC	[yaŋ] (양)	'sheep'
h. CGVC	[kwan] (관)	'crown'

(C: consonant; V: vowel; G: glide)

There are several things to be noticed about Korean syllable structure. First, mainly based on the relationship between constituents within syllables, different models of internal syllable structures have been proposed and discussed by Korean phonologists as shown in (3).

(3) Models of syllable structures in Korean

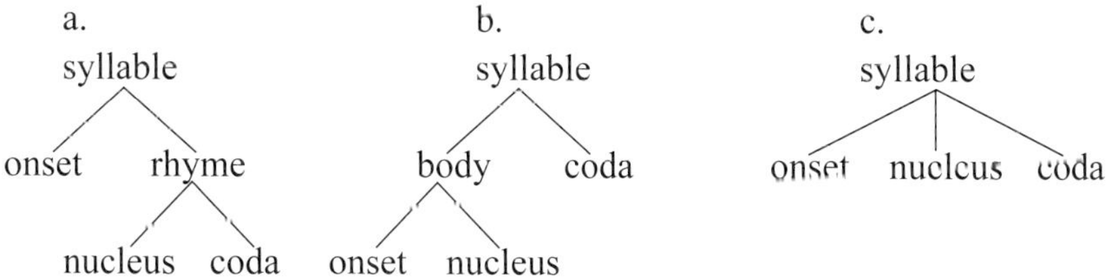

Following the claim that rhyme is a universal (e.g., Selkirk, 1978; Halle & Vergnaud, 1980), (3a) is the generally accepted model for Korean syllable structure (B-G. Kim, 1982; S-C. Kim, 1985; H-Y. Kim, 1998, C-W. Kim & H-Y. Kim, 1991; H-S. Sohn, 1987). However, based on external evidence from linguistic change, first and second language acquisition, speech errors, language games, child phonology, loan words, and misperception experiments, the syllable type in (3b) is another strongly suggested model for Korean (B-G. Lee, 1982; C-K. Gim, 1987; S-C. Ahn, 1989; C-H. Kim, 1990; K-J. Lee, 1992; Y-S. Lee, 1994; S-Y. Cheon, 2002). In addition, a flat syllable structure has been proposed indicating that there is no closer relationship between onset and nucleus or between nucleus and coda as in (3c) (Kim-Renuad, 1974; K-O. Kim & Shibatani, 1976).

Second, the status of glides[8] in Korean syllable structure has been controversial because they can be treated as either a part of the nucleus (Kim-Renaud, 1974; H-S. Sohn, 1987; C-W. Kim & H-Y. Kim, 1991) or a part of the onset (B-G. Lee, 1982; C-K. Gim, 1987; S-C. Ahn, 1989; C-H. Kim, 1990; Y-S. Lee, 1994; S-Y. Cheon, 2002). (4) shows a schematic representation of these two approaches to Korean glides.

(4) Two approaches to Korean glides

a. glides as onset
(*Onset Hypothesis*)

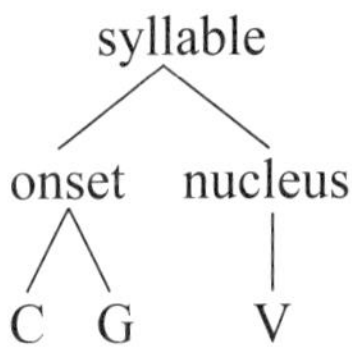

b. glides as nucleus
(*Nucleus Hypothesis*)

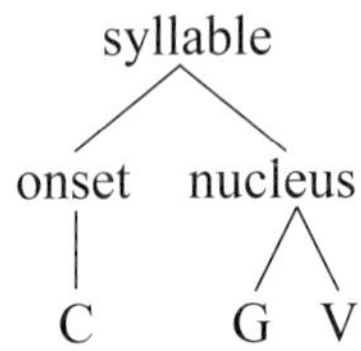

Traditional analysis treats Korean glides as vowels mainly due to the Korean orthographic representation of glides. Syllable-initially, however, when a glide comes before vowel, it behaves like a consonant (as in (1)c and (2)g). If we take a stance that a glide is considered as a consonant, then we need to answer the problem of syllable-initial consonant clusters (as shown in (2)h), which is in conflict with the syllable structure constraints. Since the detailed analysis of the status of glide in Korean is beyond the purpose of this book, I will not go into

8 Unlike English, glides in Korean are on-glides except [ɨi] ‘의’.

it any further.[9]

Syllabification in Korean

For syllabification in Korean, K-O. Kim & Shibatani (1976) propose two different syllabification rules: 1) constituent syllabification based on grammatical information, 2) segment syllabification based on surface phonetic constraints. In (5) the applications of two different syllabification rules are shown.

(5) Two syllabifications in Korean (adapted from S.-C. Ahn 1999, p. 76)

/noks/ + /ops/ + /ta/		'to stand in a daze'
'soul'	'be absent'	declarative ending
$ noks	$ opsta $	constituent syllabification
$ nok	$ opsta $	coda consonant cluster simplification
$ nok	$ ops $ ta $	segment syllabification
$ nok	$ op $ ta $	coda consonant cluster simplification
$ no	$ kop $ ta $	segment syllabification
[no.kop.t'a]		tensification and other rules

Kim-Renaud (1978) criticizes K-O. Kim and Shibatani (1976) in that they posit $opsta$ which cannot be acceptable as a syllable. S-C. Ahn (1985, 1986) proposes syllabification in Korean based on a few principles: "1) a segment string is mapped onto the CV-tier and a syllabic nucleus is assigned to every vowel (through nucleus projection) and, 2) as CV syllable structure is the most preferred type, Korean follows the *Onset First Principle*[10] (Clements & Keyser, 1983) in syllabification" (S-C. Ahn, 1999, p. 77). Thus, the Korean segmental strings of VCV

9 For a recent argument on glides in Korean, see S-Y. Cheon (2002).

10 The Onset First Principle (Clements & Keyser 1983, p. 37)

a. Syllable-initial consonants are maximized to the extent consistent with the syllable structure condition of the language in question.

b. Subsequently, syllable-final consonants are maximized to the extent consistent with the syllable structure conditions of the language in question.

are parsed into V-CV, rather than VC-V, due to the preference of CV syllable structures conforming to the Onset First Principle.

It should be noted that the syllabification (or segmentation) processes and syllable structure constraints in Korean that are discussed in this book consider the phonetic surface level only.

Korean Orthography

Orthographies differ in the degree of complexity in the relationship between print and sound: 1) shallow and 2) deep orthographies. In shallow orthographies, the correspondence between print and sound is transparent and regular (e.g. Spanish, Italian, Serbo-Croatian). On the other hand, deep orthographies characterize languages in which the mapping between print and sound is opaque in that there are many inconsistencies in spelling-to-sound rules (e.g., Hebrew and Chinese).

Table 1.2. Summary of writing system in world languages

	Script name	**Region of use**
Meaning based: Logographic	 Sinograms Kanji **Hanja**	 China, Taiwan Japan **Korea**
Syllable-based: Syllabary Alphabetic-syllabary	 Kana **Hangul**	 Japan **Korea**
Phoneme-based: Consonantal Alphabet Roman Alphabet a. Transparent b. Opaque Cyrillic Greek	 Arabic, Hebrew Spanish, Finnish English Russian, Serbian Greek	 Middle East/Africa Europe, Americas Eastern Europe Greece

Based on the segmentation of individual words in continuous speech and the representation of them, writing systems can be classified into three general types: 1) logographic, 2) syllabic, and 3) alphabetic. Table 1.2 summarizes some writing systems in terms of the written symbols which are based on different linguistic units in the world languages (adapted from Birch, 2002, p. 14).

Korean is unique because it uses both the syllable-based alphabetic-syllabary *Hangul* and the meaning-based logographic scripts *Hanja*[11] in its writing system.[12] Since the current book concerns the representation of syllabification of English words employing Korean *Hangul*, it is important to look further into this writing system.

The Korean Alphabet

The invention of the Korean Alphabet, originally called *Hunmin chong-um* (Correct Sounds for the Instruction of the People) was announced at the end of the lunar year in late 1443 or January 1444. The script was promulgated in 1446 by King Sejong (1418-1450), the fourth monarch and the revered ruler of the Chosun Kingdom, or Yi dynasty (1392-1910), whose reign was marked by an extraordinary level of cultural and scientific development (see Kim-Renaud, 1992).

The invention of the Korean alphabet was based on a limited number of principles. First, consonant letter shapes were based on kinesthetic observation of the shape of various speech organs. In addition, the letters were produced in a two-stage process in which a number of basic letters were designed first, then the remaining letters were derived from the basic letter forms. Of the seventeen consonant letters, five were created as the basic letters from which the remaining twelve letters were derived by adding strokes to the basic letters. Some examples of Korean consonants are shown in (6).

---

11 Hanja is basically logographic Chinese characters with pronunciations that differ from original Chinese pronunciations and instead follow Korean phonology.

12 Regarding the frequency of the use of scripts, the alphabetic script *Hangul* is used more often than the logographic script *Hanja* even though these scripts are used with the same text (cf. Kim & Davis, 2001).

(6) Invention of Korean consonants
(adapted from I-S. Lee, S-O., Lee and Chae, 1997)

a. Some examples of letter shapes for consonants

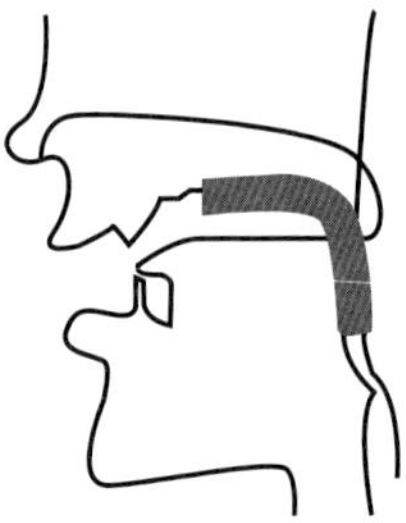

velar [k]

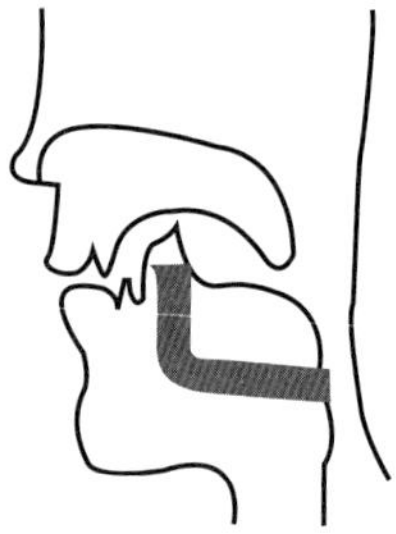

apical [n]

b. Derivation of consonants from basic consonant shapes

basic form		**derived form (1)**		**derived form (2)**
ㄱ [k]	→	ㅋ [kʰ]		
ㄴ [n]	→	ㄷ [t]	→	ㅌ [tʰ]
		↓		
		ㄹ [l]		
ㅁ [m]	→	ㅂ [p]	→	ㅍ [pʰ]
ㅅ [s]	→	ㅈ [c]	→	ㅊ [cʰ]
ㅇ [y]	→	ㆆ [ʔ]	→	ㅎ [h]

The shapes of the three basic vowel letters were based on philosophical concepts symbolizing the natural pattern of the *three great powers* of the Confucian universe: 1) *Heaven, Earth* and *Man*. Similar to the way in which consonants were invented, the vowels were also created based on combinations of the three basic vowels as shown in (7).

(7) Invention of Korean vowels

a . Three basic vowels in Korean Hangul

vowel [a]	vowel [ɨ]	vowel [i]
symbol of heaven	symbol of Earth	symbol of Man

b. Derivations of vowels from the three basic vowels (adapted I-S. Lee, S-O., Lee and Chae, 1997)

Derivation 1					**Derivation 2**				
'·'	+	'ㅡ'	→	'ㅗ'[o]	'ㅣ'	+	'ㅗ'	→	'ㅛ'[yo]
'ㅣ'	+	'·'	→	'ㅏ'[a]	'ㅣ'	+	'ㅏ'	→	'ㅑ'[ya]
'ㅡ'	+	'·'	→	'ㅜ'[u]	'ㅣ'	+	'ㅜ'	→	'ㅠ'[yu]
'·'	+	'ㅣ'	→	'ㅓ'[ə]	'ㅣ'	+	'ㅓ'	→	'ㅕ'[yə]

Second, the letters are not written one after the other in a line. Rather, they are clustered such that they fit into virtual syllabic units as shown in (8).

(8) Clustering letters fitting into virtual syllabic blocks

a. CV: [ka]

C1	**V1**

가

b. CV: [ku]

C1
V1

구

c. CVC: [kan]

C1	**V2**
C3	

간

d. CVC: [kun]

C1
V2
C3

군

e. CVVC: [kw[13]an]

C1	**V2**
V1	
C3	

관

f. CVCC: [pal or pap]

C1	**V1**
C2C3	

밟

(C: consonant; V: vowel)

13 This is just based on the representation of orthography. Since the status of glide is still controversial in Korean phonology (e.g., onset approach, nucleus approach or dual status approach), and treatment of the glide argument in Korean is beyond the scope of this work, and will not be discussed in depth.

As shown, consonant and vowel are combined together fitting into invisible syllabic blocks as represented in squares above. Orthographically, the syllable onset has one consonant letter while the coda can have two consonant letters maximally as shown in (8f): The syllable has two consonant letters in the coda position while its pronunciation on the surface is either [pal] or [pab] depending on the speaker. However, when the syllable is followed by a vowel-initial syllable, the latter consonant of the two in coda position is resyllabified into the onset of the following syllable as in '밟+아' /palp/ +/a/ → [pal.ba].

Structure of The Study

The general organization of the remainder of the book is as follows:

Chapter 2 will delve deeper into native Korean speakers' segmentation strategies by replicating Treiman and Danis' (1988) two experiments: 1) syllable-detection and 2) syllable reversal tasks. The research study in Chapter 2 is both descriptive and experimental in nature, utilizing meta-linguistic manipulation games. The rationale behind employing these two experiments is to examine whether a certain segmentation strategy observed in one language can be maintained when speakers of the language parse typologically different languages. In so doing, the current chapter will test the following hypotheses:

- Hypothesis 1: The parsing strategies in a native language (L1: Korean) will be employed even in the segmentation of the target language (L2: English).
- Hypothesis 2: Even if L2 is typologically different from L1, the speakers' working knowledge of L2 will play a greater role in segmentation.
- Hypothesis 3: Along with interference from L1, interlanguage (Selinker 1969, 1972) segmentation patterns will emerge.

Hypothesis 1 is a strong approach to the L1 effect, and it predicts that there will be a strong CV-biased segmentation of English by native speakers of Korean (Lim, 2003). On the other hand, Hypothesis 2 focuses on the working knowledge of the L2 learners by predicting that the L2 knowledge will play a greater role in the parsing process, i.e., segmentation, than the L1 parsing strategy. Finally, Hypothesis 3 takes a stance that intertwines the effects of L1 with those of L2 by standing between Hypotheses 1 and 2 in terms of segmentation.

Chapter 3 will explore a typological relationship between segmentation and syllable counting. Languages may differ in the degree to which syllable boundaries are clear or ambiguous. Interestingly, English speakers seem to be able to say how many syllables are contained in a given word without much difficulty, but have more difficulty in saying where each syllable begins or ends: For example, does the word-medial /m/ in 'lemon' belong to the first, or second syllable, or to both? (cf. Abercrombie, 1967). When it comes to denoting these syllable boundaries in Korean, however, Korean speakers seem to have a clearer understanding of the syllable divisions (e.g., they would unanimously say that the /m/ in 'lemon' belongs to the second syllable of the word). Korean speakers, though, tend to inconsistently count syllable numbers in English words (e.g., their answers would vary as to how many syllables there are in words such as 'acid' and 'cake'). In order to examine these dynamics and relationships between segmentation and syllable counting, I will probe the patterns of the Korean speakers' syllable counts of English words by closely examining how Koreans represent English words using Korean orthography. The motivation for choosing Korean orthography as the object of the current chapter is two-fold:

- Korean is transparent in terms of mapping sounds onto letters such that the relationship between spoken and written representations of speech is relatively straightforward and the representations are faithful to one other.

- The Korean orthographic representation is visually syllable-based: Each syllable should be expressed within a virtual syllabic block.

The relationship between orthography and L1/L2 perception will be discussed in further detail in Chapter 6.

Based on the findings in Chapter 3 along with the segmentation strategies reported in Chapter 2, I will propose that the CV-Syllable Structure consists of segmentation units (or rhythmic units) in Korean. Furthermore, following Erickson, Akahane-Yamada, Tajima and Matsumoto's (1999) assertion that "rhythm is considered a central organizing factor in speech perception and production," I will also discuss the possibility that different rhythmic units may lead to different perception of L2 syllables and voicing contrasts by L1 speakers.

In Chapters 2 and 3, it is speculated that the rhythm-based units in language are the basic units not only for segmentation but also for perception (cf. Cutler, Mehler, Norris & Segui, 1986). In Chapters 4 and 5, I will employ a new paradigm - *a repetitive speech task* - (Stetson, 1951), in order to interrogate the relationship between segmentation and perception under systematically varied conditions. Specifically, I will replicate previous studies (Lim, de Jong & Nagao, 2001; Nagao, Lim, & de Jong, 2001) in order to scrutinize the hypothesis that the CV-Syllable Structure is the basic unit for perception as well as segmentation by Korean learners of English.

Chapter 4 will lay out the general methodology of repetitive speech tasks in which perception of repetitive speech is meticulously examined in order to probe perceptual patterns of dynamic modulation of syllable structure as a function of speech rate (de Jong 2001a, 2001b). With a thorough examination of the perceptual patterns of 23 native speakers of Midwest English, Chapter 4 will serve as the baseline experiment for further inquiries in Chapters 5 and 6.

Chapter 5 will investigate second language learners' perceptual patterns of English syllable affiliation and voicing contrasts. It will also seek to understand effects of the degree of exposure to the L2 on perception in repetitive speech by examining two different L2 learner groups in terms of their degree of L2 exposure: 1) Korean learners who have had more exposure to English, having spent at least one semester studying English in the United States; and 2) Korean learners less exposed to English, having learned English only in their home country. In Chapter 5, I will argue that the CV structure-based segmentation strategies used by Koreans become more evident in the perception of repetitive speech in English. I will also report the positive effects of Koreans' L2 exposure on their L2 perception.

This chapter will also move deeper into the process of decoding continuous speech from the perspective of second language learning. In second language learning, for instance, Korean learners of English may have to attend more to allophones and segmentation in English, which will eventually lead them to a better approximation of native-like stress patterns and phrasal rhythms (cf. Trammell, 1999). In this chapter, I will examine effects of language background on learning of the segmentation of an L2. I will also show how the experiments employed throughout the previous chapters are tied to this process. Furthermore, based on Flege's Speech Learning Model (Flege, 1995, 1998, 1999, 2002, 2003), I will propose a new model for bilinguals.

Chapter 6 will expand our understanding of how speakers' knowledge of orthographies, either native or target languages, affects perception of segmentation and voicing contrasts in the repetitive speech production of English. Orthographies differ in terms of the degree of complexity in a language regarding the relationship between print and sound: 1) shallow and 2) deep orthographies (cf. Birch, 2002). In shallow orthographies, the correspondence between print and sound is transparent and regular (e.g., Spanish, Italian, and Serbo-Croatian). On the other hand, deep orthographies characterize languages in which the mapping between print and sound is opaque in that there are many inconsistencies in spelling-to-sound rules (e.g., Hebrew and Chinese). In Chapter 6, I will suggest that Korean orthography is a good reflex of phonology, and thus, it will affect perception of a second language.

Chapter 7 will summarize this book's major findings and arguments, and will also consider how they contribute to the issues concerning segmentation, particularly the production, perception, orthography, and second language learning processes of segmentation. The final chapter will also discuss the significance of the book for linguists' and other scholars' understanding of segmentation as well as perception of voicing contrasts; this will be accompanied by questions and suggestions for further investigation.

CHAPTER 2

SEGMENTATION STRATEGIES BY KOREAN LEARNERS

Introduction

It is well known that French has relatively simple syllable structures and straightforward syllabification. For example, native speakers of French easily syllabify a French word 'facile' with a syllable boundary placed between 'fa-' and '-cile' (cf. Content et al., 2001). The language has predominantly open syllable types, i.e., CV syllable structures, (Goldman et al., 1996) and has no lexically contrastive stress. Korean is also known to have simpler syllable structures than English, and its syllabification is as straightforward as in French. Like French, the Korean CV syllable structure has a special status in Korean in that syllabification of VCV words in Korean is typically made into the V-CV segmentation on the phonetic surface level (cf. K-O. Kim & Shibatani, 1976; S-C. Ahn, 1985, 1986, 1998) regardless of its two different orthographic representations in Korean as in (1a) and (1b).

(1) V-CV syllabification of two different orthographic representations on the phonetic level in Korean

orthographic representation	phonetic representation	gloss
a. CVC̲#V: ka**k**#o (각#오)	[ka.**k**o (가.고)]	'resolution'
b. CV#C̲V: ka#**k**o (가#고)	[ka.**k**o (가.고)]	'go and⋯'

(#: morpheme boundary; . : syllable boundary)

In contrast, the English syllabification of intervocalic consonants, on the surface level, is heavily affected by vowel quality (Pulgram, 1970), speech rate (Kahn, 1976), and the phonetic natures of intervocalic consonants (Treiman & Danis, 1988). Consequently, English speakers tend to show inconsistent syllabification patterns of intervocalic consonants. In an attempt to understand these inconsistences, Treiman and Danis (1988) found that sonority is one of the major factors in this context, *ambisyllabification*: The more sonorous intervocalic consonants (i.e., VCV) are, the more likely they are to be treated as ambisyllabic. Another factor is the effect of spelling on syllabification. Treiman and Danis (1988) reported that English speakers were more likely to place an intervocalic consonant into both the preceding and following syllables if they thought that the consonant was spelled with a double letter than if they thought it was spelled with a single letter. They therefore suggest that double consonants may promote the ambisyllabicity of intervocalic consonants.

Extending these findings to the study of the French language, Content et al. (2001) tested the generality of the role of sonority and spelling in syllabification using French. They found that while the syllabification in French was also influenced by sonority, the spelling effect was actually much larger than in English. They also noted that more predominant CV responses on the second syllables are found in French than English.

Syllabification of Intervocalic Consonants in Second Language Learning

The question of ambisyllabic consonants in English has had a long history in theoretical linguistics (cf. Vennemann, 1988). However, investigating this ambisyllabicity from the perspective of second language acquisition is a fairly recent development. In studies of syllable structure transfer in interlanguage phonology, Tarone (1984) and Broselow (1984) were concerned with this ambisyllabicity of English consonants, mainly focusing on phrase-level ambisyllabicity with relevance to a universal preference for CV syllables in interlanguage. In a study on English ambisyllabic consonants, Trammell (1999) emphasized the importance of word-level ambisyllabicity in second language learning:

> We believe that attention to ambisyllabic articulations will produce more native-like allophones and syllabification, which in turn will lead to a better approximation of English stress patterns and, hence, phrasal rhythm, because syllabification is intimately tied to syllable weight, which plays a large role in stress assignment. (p.325)

He claims that "the habit of English ambisyllabification may also be relevant to the non-native speakers' problem of lengthening and clearly articulating unstressed vowels" (p. 328). This could be a reasonable explanation of Korean learners' tendency to stress every single vowel in English words creating a "staccato effect." Trammell stressed the importance of the teaching and developing students' awareness of ambisyllabification, especially in regards to the different prosodic level:

> Students of EFL will be more likely to produce the correct word-level stress patterns in the L2, if they syllabify correctly; and that in turn will help them with the allophones of the segmental phonemes and in the production of correct phrase- and sentence-level rhythm and intonation patterns that are so important in communication. (p. 334)

Hypotheses

The purpose of this chapter is to examine whether a certain syllabification strategy observed in one language (L1) can be maintained when speakers of the language are parsing typologically different languages (L2, L3···). To that end, we specifically examined the syllabification patterns of intervocalic English consonants by Korean speakers whose L1 syllabification strategy shows a strong V-CV division of VCV words. As mentioned earlier, syllabification of intervocalic consonants in English, in general, is affected by stress placement, spelling, and categories of intervocalic consonants (Treiman & Danis, 1988). Assuming the strong CV-preference in syllabification of intervocalic consonants shown in Korean, then, these factors for English syllabification by native speakers of English may not be significant factors in syllabification of English by

Korean speakers. Alternatively, as in the case of English syllabification of intervocalic consonants reported by Treiman and Danis (1988), these factors may play a great role in English syllabification by Koreans, as well. Accordingly, the current chapter is designed to examine whether or not Korean speakers use the same parsing strategies to syllabify English words as they do in Korean syllabification.

This chapter aims to answer the following questions:

1. Is a certain syllabification strategy of Korean (L1), *a strong V-**C**V syllabification preference*, also maintained in parsing English (L2) words?

2. To what extent do the three significant factors in English syllabification manifested by native speakers of English, *categories of intervocalic consonants, stress placement,* and *spelling*, affect Korean (L1) speakers' syllabification in English (L2) words?

These two research questions above were examined to investigate the following hypotheses:

- **Hypothesis 1**: The parsing strategies in a native language (L1), here, *Korean*, will be employed even in the syllabification of the target language (L2), *English*.
- **Hypothesis 2**: Even if the target language (L2, *English*) is typologically different from native language (L1, *Korean*), participants' working knowledge of the L2 will play a major role in syllabification of English words (to some extent).
- **Hypothesis 3**: Along with interference from L1 (Korean), interlanguage syllabification patterns will emerge.

Hypothesis 1 is a strong approach to the L1 (Korean) effect and it predicts that there will be a strong CV-biased syllabification in English by native speakers of Korean. On the other hand, Hypothesis 2 focuses on the working knowledge of the learner of an L2 (English) by predicting that the L2 knowledge will play a greater role in the parsing process than the CV-biased L1 parsing strategy. Therefore, it predicts that syllabification patterns similar to those reported in Treiman and Danis (1988) will emerge since the Korean learners' working knowledge of English is expected to take over and replace the native, *Korean*, CV-based syllabification. Finally, Hypothesis 3 combines the effects of L1 (Korean) and those of L2 (English). As a result, it presents a view of L2 syllabification that is somewhat between H1 and H2 in terms of syllabification. This, basically, stems from the nature of an interlanguage in which we can find a mixture of L1 and L2, or unique patterns which are observed neither in L1 nor in L2.

Experiment 1

Methods

If Korean speakers have a strong tendency to syllabify CV<u>C</u>V Korean words into CV-CV forms, they would do the same even when they parse words in languages other than their native tongue (i.e., sofa → 'so-fa'; mama → 'ma-ma'). That is, they would not notice the relationships between stress placement and spelling when parsing words in English but would instead rely on the same strategies used in Korean. Therefore, we would expect to see a different outcome from that in Treiman and Danis's (1988) study. Korean speakers would not rely on the phonetic nature of intervocalic consonants when parsing English words, but rather, the strong CV-preference in syllabification pattern in Korean may play a major role in English syllabification.

Alternatively, if Korean speakers use different strategies in their English syllabification because the language in question is not their mother tongue, they may not only rely on their knowledge of English parsing, but also develop a novel skill different from Korean syllabification such that their parsing strategies will be significantly different from those used in their own language (L1, *Korean*). In other words, their parsing strategies may be closer to those of English speakers. If that is the case, we can expect to see similar syllabification patterns in English by Koreans to those reported in Treiman and Danis (1988).

To examine these different scenarios, Experiment 1 was designed to see whether the syllabification strategy in Korean would also operate in the syllabification process in English. To that end, Experiment 1 investigated the performance of Korean-speaking learners of English in a syllable-detection task using English words.

Participants: The Younger Generation

Twenty-one native speakers (7 males and 14 females) of Standard Korean participated in Experiment 1. They were all college students at a university[14] in the Seoul area: The participants were all recruited from elective courses at the university, and were paid 10 dollars[15] for their participation. As shown in Table 2.1, this study controls for the age factor by using young native speakers of Standard Korean — aged from 19 through 25 — in order to minimize the variation in responses due to age differences. At the same time this maximizes the understanding of syllabification patterns by younger people. They were not aware of the purpose of the experiment, nor had they received any explicit phonetic training.

Table 2.1. Participant information

<table>
<tr><th rowspan="2"></th><th rowspan="2">number</th><th colspan="4">age</th></tr>
<tr><th colspan="2">mean</th><th colspan="2">minimum – maximum</th></tr>
<tr><td>male</td><td>7 (33.3%)</td><td>24yrs</td><td rowspan="2">22.95yrs</td><td>22-25yrs</td><td rowspan="2">19-25yrs</td></tr>
<tr><td>female</td><td>14 (66.7%)</td><td>22.43yrs</td><td>19-24yrs</td></tr>
</table>

Monolingual vs. Bilingual?

I also controlled the degree to which participants have been exposed to English because the current study is primarily designed to focus on *monolinguals*, who use the national language, here, *Standard Korean*, to function in their everyday lives, not on *bilinguals* or *multilinguals*.[16]

The question of how to define bilingualism or multilingualism has engaged researchers for a very long time. According to Bloomfield (1933), bilingualism results from the addition of a perfectly learned foreign language to one's own, undiminished native tongue. However, 'perfection' in his definition is relative. On the contrary, Macnamara (1967) proposes that a bilingual is anyone who possesses a minimal competence in one of the four language skills, i.e. listening comprehension, speaking, reading, and writing in a language other than his or her mother tongue. In a more basic understanding of bilingualism, Weinreich (1953) defined bilingualism as the alternate use of two languages. It is clear that some researchers have favored a narrow definition of bilingualism and argued that only those individuals who possess language skills in two languages very similar to those of a monolingual should be considered bilingual. More recently, however, researchers who study bilingual and multilingual communities around the world have argued for a broad definition that views bilingualism as a common human condition that makes it possible for an individual to function, at some level, in more than one language. Edwards (1994), however, argues that this broader sense proves to be unsatisfactory. He adds that most modern treatments of bilingualism acknowledge that any meaningful discussion of bilingualism or multilingualism must be

---

14 Many thanks go to Prof. Jinyong Tak for generously helping recruit students as participants.

15 Since the experiment was conducted in Korea, the payment was made in their own currency, 'won' (cf. the exchange rates at the time of payment: 1 dollar = 1020.62 won)

16 For further definitions and arguments on bilingualism or multingualism, see Appel & Muysken (1987), Grosjean (1982), Hamers & Blanc (1989), Weinreich (1974).

attempted within a specific context, and for specific purposes. But, he does concede that a "vast number of those to whom the term 'bilingual' can be at all reasonably applied fall into the category of 'non-fluent' bilingualism"(p. 58).

If I take the broad definition of bilinguals in my study, it will be very difficult to recruit monolinguals from the college student population because every Korean college student generally has some level of English proficiency. For example, considering that college entrance exams would likely screen out students without some level of English proficiency,[17] it seems difficult to categorize these college students as monolinguals. Furthermore, given that English education in Korea starts in the elementary schools[18] and private tutoring in English is available even for pre-school children, it would be almost impossible to find monolinguals, in the broad sense, among college students. Therefore, the current study takes a stance towards the narrow sense of bilingualism. The study used college students who have little or no experience living in English-speaking countries, so they were expected to have little exposure to spoken English, especially American English.

Participants' Self-Rating of Their English Proficiency

Even though it was not my main concern to rate the participants' English proficiency for the purpose of the current study, it was necessary to exclude experienced or advanced learners of English, in order to avoid

17 Current College Entrance Exams in South Korea include several academic subjects such as Korean, English, Math, and others; as far as English exams are concerned, the exams test two areas of English skills: 1) listening and 2) reading comprehension. Strictly speaking, though, the college entrance exams cannot be a direct measure of English proficiency skills even though the proportion of English in the entrance exams carries more weight than any other subject.

18 The government-mandated English education at elementary schools was officially launched in 1997 and the School English Education is mainly based on communicative approaches to the English language. The Ministry of Education mandates that the start of English education should be the third-grade. After a decade of this mandatory English education in elementary schools, the Korean government considers extending its mandatory English education as early as the first-graders.

any possibility that the results may not come directly from the participants' native syllabification patterns but from their high English proficiency[19]. To that end, I screened participants through brief one-on-one oral interviews asking about their background in English education and their degree of exposure to spoken American English. After selecting participants who met my criteria, I asked them to self-rate their English proficiency using questionnaires. Following are the survey results of participants' self-evaluation of their English proficiency in terms of four basic language skills: 1) Reading, 2) Writing, 3) Listening, and 4) Speaking.

Figure 2.1. Participants' self-evaluation on their English proficiency

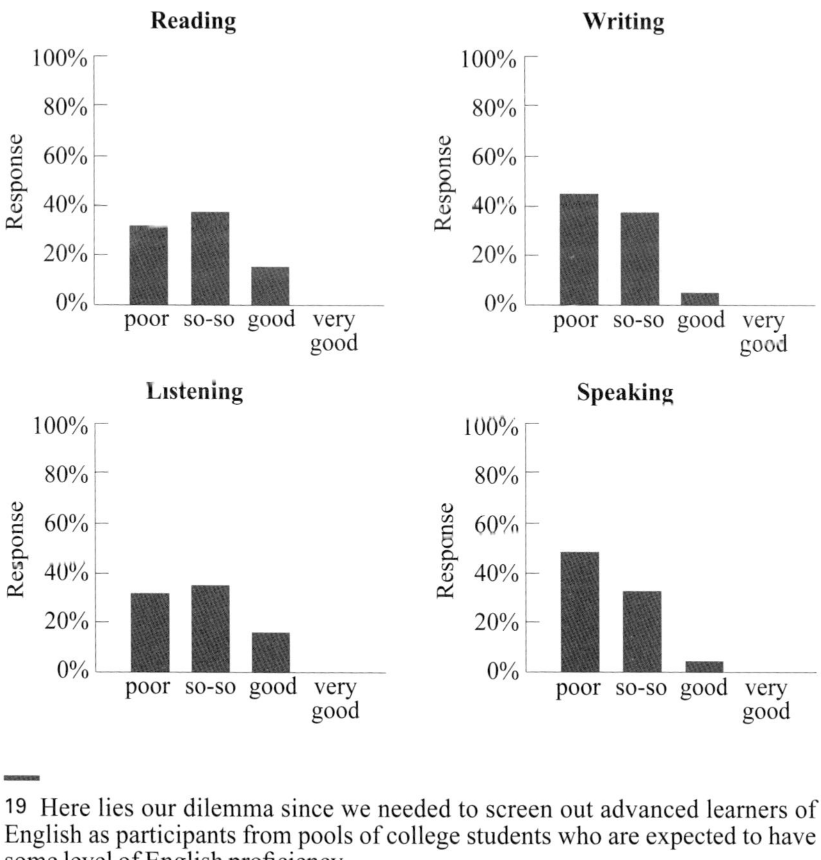

19 Here lies our dilemma since we needed to screen out advanced learners of English as participants from pools of college students who are expected to have some level of English proficiency.

Participants rated their English proficiency in four different areas, *reading, writing, listening, and speaking*, by selecting one of four different choices to describe their English proficiency — two negative ones (*poor* and *so-so*) and two positive ones (*good* and *very good*).As shown in Figure 2.1, results showed that most participants rated their English proficiency negatively all across the four areas; with negative responses of Reading (81%), Writing (95%), Listening (81%), and Speaking (95%).

Interestingly, participants felt relatively most confident of their English reading ability when they were asked to indicate their strongest English skills, which for this question included English grammar as a possible choice. These results are shown in Figure 2.2.

Figure 2.2. Korean participants' confidence in their English skills

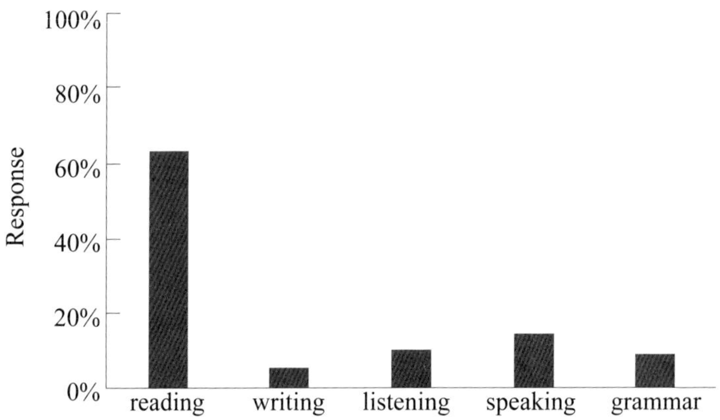

Given that the traditional method of English education in Korea focuses on reading comprehension and grammar, it is not surprising to see that the participants felt most confident in their reading skills in English (62%). However, it is surprising to see such low confidence in Grammar (10%).

It should be noted that none of the above self-ratings should be viewed as objective measures of the participant proficiency in English due to possible inaccuracies and difficulties of self-assessment. Rather, they can be used as an indirect indicator as to how the participants in my study felt about themselves and their attitude toward the English language in a general sense.

In sum, the 21 participants (7 males and 14 females) who participated in this study were all college students and had little or no exposure to spoken American English outside of classroom or tutoring settings. Self-evaluation of their English proficiency showed us that the participants were not confident in their English ability in four basic areas, *reading, writing, listening,* and *speaking*, even though they already have enough English proficiency to pass college entrance exams[20]. The participants showed especially low confidence in spoken language skills, i.e., listening and speaking in English. Further explanation of the Korean participants' attitude toward English will be given in the discussion sections.

Stimulus Materials

Stimuli for Experiment 1 were 84 mono-morphemic bisyllabic English words with a single intervocalic consonant. The words were chosen with variations of 1) consonant category, 2) stress placement, and 3) spelling of intervocalic consonants in CV<u>C</u>V environments as shown below.

(2) Variations within CV<u>C</u>V words

a. **Stress** placement:
1) first syllable vs. 2) second syllable

b. **Category** of intervocalic consonants:
1) obstruents[21] 2) nasals 3) liquids

c. **Spellings** of intervocalic consonants:
1) single 2) double

---

20 Korean College Entrance Exams are composite in nature; therefore, they do not necessarily indicate each examinee's levels in specific subjects such as English or math as pointed out in Footnote 17. In my study, however, I simply assume that college students have some level of English proficiency.

21 Here, this includes only stops and fricatives.

That is, the stimuli were grouped into three different categories of intervocalic consonants: 1) obstruents, 2) nasals, and 3) liquids. In half of the words within each group, the intervocalic consonant was spelled by a single letter and the other half by two identical letters. In addition, stress placement was on either the first or the second syllables. As mentioned, all stimuli we used were two-syllable English words[22]. Some examples[23] are shown in (3).

(3) Some example-stimuli for Experiment 1

consonant category	**stress placement**	**spelling**	**word**
obstruent	first	single	to**p**ic, e**v**er
nasal	first	single	le**m**on, pa**n**ic
liquid	first	single	me**l**on, E**r**ic
obstruent	second	single	de**p**end, re**v**eal
nasal	second	single	de**m**and, de**n**y
liquid	second	single	se**l**ect, e**r**ase
obstruent	first	double	ra**bb**it, Be**tt**y
nasal	first	double	co**mm**a, te**nn**is
liquid	first	double	ba**ll**ot, bo**rr**ow
obstruent	second	double	su**pp**ort, su**ff**ice
nasal	second	double	co**mm**and, co**nn**ect
liquid	second	double	co**ll**ect, co**rr**ect

(Cf. Intervocalic consonants are bold-faced and stressed vowels are underlined)

All the stimulus materials were recorded with a clear-speech-style[24] spoken in isolation by a male native speaker of American English from

22 All English words we used are real words; they were nouns and verbs including some common proper names like Eric and Helen.

23 For exhaustive lists of the stimuli, see Appendix A.

24 This speech style is defined subjectively. For the current study, however, the speaker was asked to read the lists as clearly as possible and also to avoid lapsing into a mechanical speech pattern.

Michigan.[25] The stimuli were randomized, divided into four blocks, and recorded with a Sonymicrophone directly onto digital audiotapes in the recording-room of the Linguistics Department at Indiana University. Stimuli were separated by approximately 3 seconds of silence using the speech editing software *Cool Edit 2000*.

Procedure

The task of Experiment 1[26] was relatively simple. Participants heard the recorded and were asked to write each English words they heard using Korean. The reasoning for using Korean orthography is that, unlike English, Korean orthography shows a clear boundary between morphemes since each vowel and consonant are combined such that each morpheme fits into a syllable-based unit. Therefore, it was expected that this written task would show the syllabification process of Korean participants straightforwardly. The participants showed no difficulty with the task through a warm-up session of five sample words. The order of presentation of the four blocks was randomized for each participant. The experiment was conducted individually with twenty-one participants using a personal laptop computer in a quiet room.

After the task was completed, the participants were asked to write down each word using English orthography in order to ascertain that they knew the standard English spelling of the intervocalic consonants.

---

25 The speaker was born and grew up in the Mid-Western Area. He was 24 years old at the time of recording and had no history of speech or hearing related problems.

26 The task was originally designed to obtain the participants' oral responses; however, it turned out that participants felt very uncomfortable with the task since they thought that the purpose of the task was to rate their pronunciation of English. Therefore, they were very hesitant to do the oral task. In addition, once they thought they made a mistake in the oral task, they were troubled with the mistakes, which seemed to affect their further performance. Since the object of the experiment was not to rate the participants' English pronunciation, I decided to ask them only to write down in Korean, instead, since I felt that their discomfort with the oral task might affect the results to some extent.

Experiment 1: Results

Syllabification of English Intervocalic Consonants by Koreans

Results were analyzed based on a total of 1764 responses (84 words * 21 participants) from the written task in Experiment 1. I examined and coded the responses in terms of whether the intervocalic consonants of the words belong to 1) the first syllable (coded as V**C**-V) or 2) the second syllable (coded as V-**C**V) or 3) both syllables (coded as V**C**-**C**V) or 4) if for any reason, none of these categories were applicable, the response was coded as Error (Here, for instance, segments with more than two major featural differences from English segments were marked as errors). The syllabification patterns of English consonants by native speakers of Korean are shown in Figure 2.3.

Figure 2.3. Syllabification of English intervocalic consonants by Koreans (Exp.1)

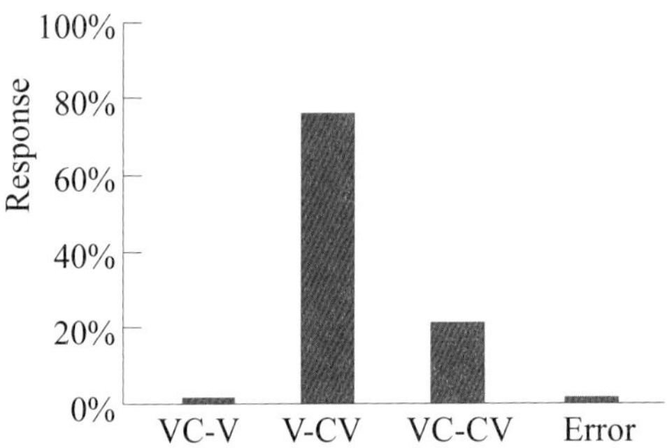

It seems that most native speakers of Korean syllabify English intervocalic consonants as the onset of the second syllable (encoded as V-**C**V as shown). In addition, there were relatively significant portions of ambisyllabic (or belonging to both syllables)-syllabification responses (V**C**-**C**V). That is, the participants responded that the intervocalic consonants in question belong to both syllables, as a coda to the preceding syllable and as an onset to the following syllable simultaneously. However, interestingly, almost no responses were observed for V**C**-V syllabification in which the intervocalic consonant served only as the codas of the preceeding.

A general picture of the syllabification of English intervocalic consonants by Korean participants shows that there seems to be a strong preference for V-CV syllabification in that quite a substantial portion of responses (77%) showed that the intervocalic consonants in English words were syllabified as an onset to the following, or second, syllables in (C)VCV(C) environments. In addition, as much as 21% of the responses showed ambisyllabic (i.e., VC-CV) syllabification of the intervocalic consonants. In the following sub-sections, then, I will look further into the effects of the consonant category, stress placement, and spellings of intervocalic consonants on syllabification in detail.

Effects of Consonant Category on Syllabification

I first turn to consonant category effect on syllabification. Table 2.2 shows the tabulation of syllabification and consonant category.

Table 2.2. Cross-tabulations of syllabification and consonant category (Exp. 1)

consonant category	**syllabification**				
	VC-V	**V-CV**	**VC-CV**	**error**	**total**
obstruents	0	585(99.5%)	0	3(0.5%)	588
nasals	11(1.9%)	567(96.5%)	2 (0.3%)	8(1.3%)	588
liquids	10(1.8%)	199(33.8%)	366(62.2%)	13(2.2%)	588
total	**21(1.1%)**	**1351(76.6%)**	**368(20.9%)**	**24(1.4%)**	**1764**

As shown in Table 2.2, there seems to be a large effect of consonant category on syllabification ($x^2 = 946.54$, df $= 6$, $p < 0.005$). That is, 99% (585/588) of intervocalic obstruents and 97% (567/588) of intervocalic nasals were syllabified as V-CV while intervocalic liquids showed a much lower percentage of V-CV syllabification (34%: 199/588). Instead, interestingly, a higher percentage of ambisyllabic (VC-CV) responses were observed for intervocalic liquids (62%: 366/588). In the above-mentioned 21% ambisyllabic responses for intervocalic consonants almost all came in environments with intervocalic liquids (21%: 366/1764). However, a closer examination showed a split in the syllabification in liquids of the total 588 intervocalic liquids, the /l/ and the /r/ account for 71% (420/588) and 29% (168/588) respectively. The syllabification for these intervocalic liquids (/l/ and /r/) is shown in Figure 2.4.

Figure 2.4. Syllabification of intervocalic liquids by Koreans (Exp.1)

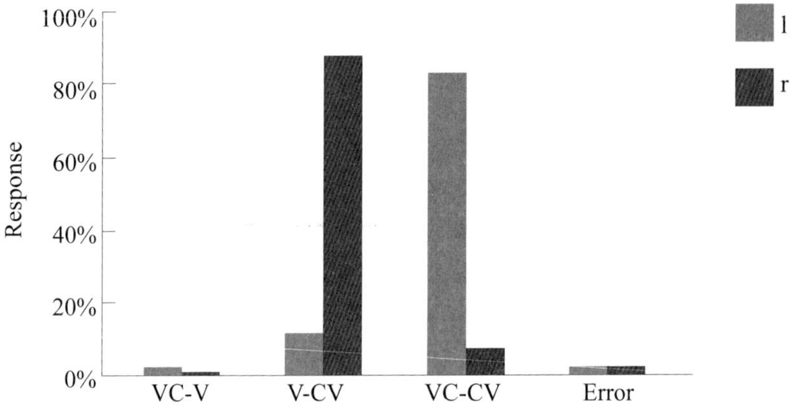

As can be seen, intervocalic liquids /l/ and /r/ are very different in terms of syllabification. The intervocalic /r/ patterns with obstruents and nasals in that they are syllabified as V-CV while almost every intervocalic /l/ is syllabified as VC-CV, i.e., ambisyllabic syllabification. It should be noted that ambisyllabic syllabification of intervocalic consonants by Korean speakers comes almost entirely from the intervocalic /l/ in my study. That is, of the total 366 ambisyllabic responses, 96% (352/368) come from the intervocalic /l/.

In summary, there seems to be a significant intervocalic consonant category effect on syllabification: The V-CV syllabification was used consistently for intervocalic consonants such as obstruents, nasals, and /r/ while /l/ was nearly always syllabified as VC-CV.

Effects of Stress Placement on Syllabification

We will now consider how stress placement in words affects which syllable an intervocalic consonant belongs to. To explore this, I used bisyllabic English words varying stress placement to fall either on the first syllable or the second syllable. Table 2.3 shows syllabification of intervocalic consonants as a function of stress placement.

Table 2.3. Syllabification of intervocalic consonants as a function of stress

stress placement	syllabification				
	VC-V	V-CV	VC-CV	error	total
1st_syllable	11(1.2%)	664(73.5%)	214(23.7%)	14(1.6%)	903
2nd_syllable	10(1.1%)	687(79.9%)	154(17.9%)	10(1.1%)	861
total	**21(1.1%)**	**1351(76.6%)**	**368(20.9%)**	**24(1.4%)**	**1764**

As shown in Table 2.3, there seems to be no effect of word-level stress placement on syllabification of English intervocalic consonants by Korean speakers in that most of the words are syllabified as V-CV regardless of the location of the stress placement. Specifically, words with first syllable stress accounted for 74% (664/903) of the intervocalic consonants syllabified as V-CV. This is followed by 24% (214/903) ambisyllabic syllabification (i.e., VC-CV). A similar proportion occurs for the words with second syllable stress: 80% (687/861) for V-CV syllabification and 18% (154/861) for VC-CV syllabification.

In the previous section, I have shown that the intervocalic /l/ is different in terms of syllabification in that it is syllabified as ambisyllabic while other intervocalic consonants are all syllabified as V-CV. So, I decided to closely look at the intervocalic liquids by varyng stress placement in the words. Figure 2.5 shows the relationship between stress placement and syllabification for the liquids /l/ and /r/.

As shown below, both intervocalic liquids /l/ and /r/ show consistent syllabification patterns whether or not stress is placed on the first or second syllable. That is, the intervocalic /l/s are consistently syllabified as ambisyllabic while the intervocalic /r/s are syllabified as V-CV regardless of stress placement.

It therefore appears that word-level stress placement does not affect Korean speakers' syllabification of English intervocalic consonants.

Figure 2.5. Syllabification of intervocalic liquids differentiated by stress-placement (Exp. 1)

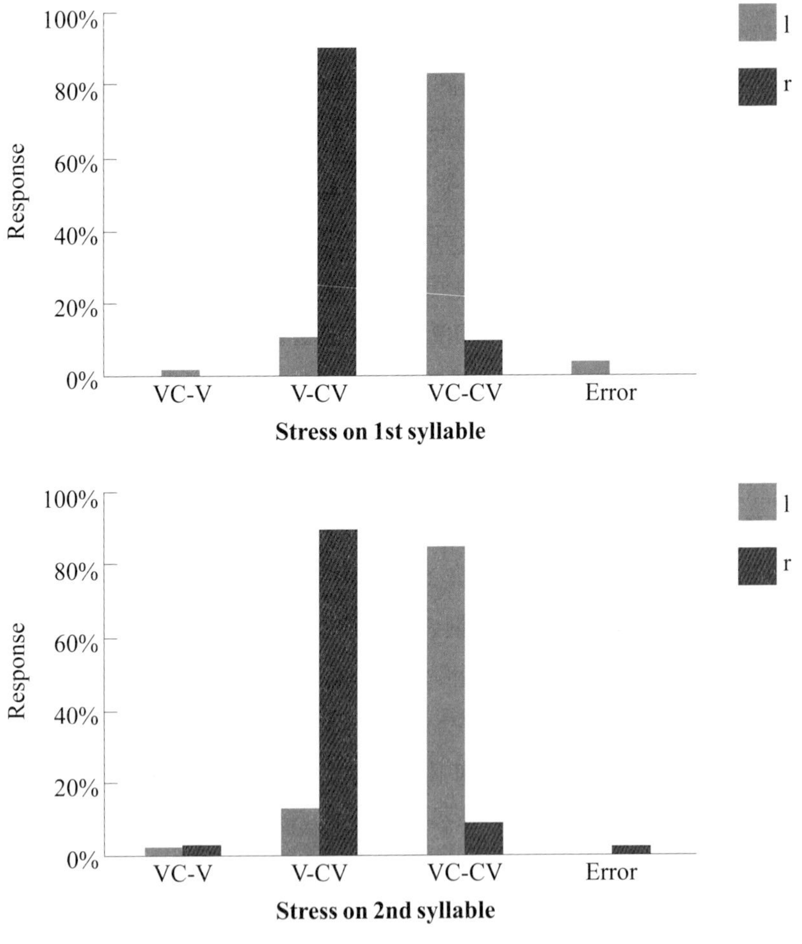

Effects of Spellings on Syllabification

Finally, I turn to the effects of spelling on the syllabification patterns in English by the native speakers of Korean. Previous studies show that English speakers are more likely to place an intervocalic consonant into both preceding and following syllables if they thought that the consonant was spelled with double letters than if they thought it was spelled with a single letter (Treiman & Danis, 1988). Considering this, my main concern in this section is to examine whether and how English spellings of intervocalic consonants in words, that is, either 1) with single letter or 2) with double letters, affect the Korean speakers' syllabification patterns in English. More specifically, I want to know if the strong V-CV syllabification pattern holds, among Korean speakers, regardless of spellings of the intervocalic consonants. The findings to this question are summarized in Table 2.4.

Table 2.4. Syllabification as a function of spelling

spelling	syllabification				
	VC-V	V-CV	VC-CV	error	total
single	13(1.4%)	649(73.6%)	201(22.8%)	19(2.2%)	882
double	8(0.9%)	702(79.6%)	167(18.9%)	5(0.6%)	882
total	**21(1.1%)**	**1351(76.6%)**	**368(20.9%)**	**24(1.4%)**	**1764**

First, the V-CV syllabification occurs 74% (649/882) of the time for the single-lettered intervocalic consonants and 80% (702/882) for the double-lettered intervocalic consonants. Secondly, some substantial numbers of VC-CV syllabification are also observed: 23%(201/882) for the single-letter consonants and 19% (167/882) for the double-letter consonants ($x^2 = 14.58$, df = 3, $p = 0.002$). Once again, however, we must recall that almost all the VC-CV syllabification comes from intervocalic/l/. Thus, if we exclude /l/ from this calculation, we can say that the strong V-CV syllabification is maintained regardless of the spellings of the intervocalic consonants as shown below.

Figure 2.6. Syllabification of intervocalic consonants differentiated by spelling (Exp. 1)

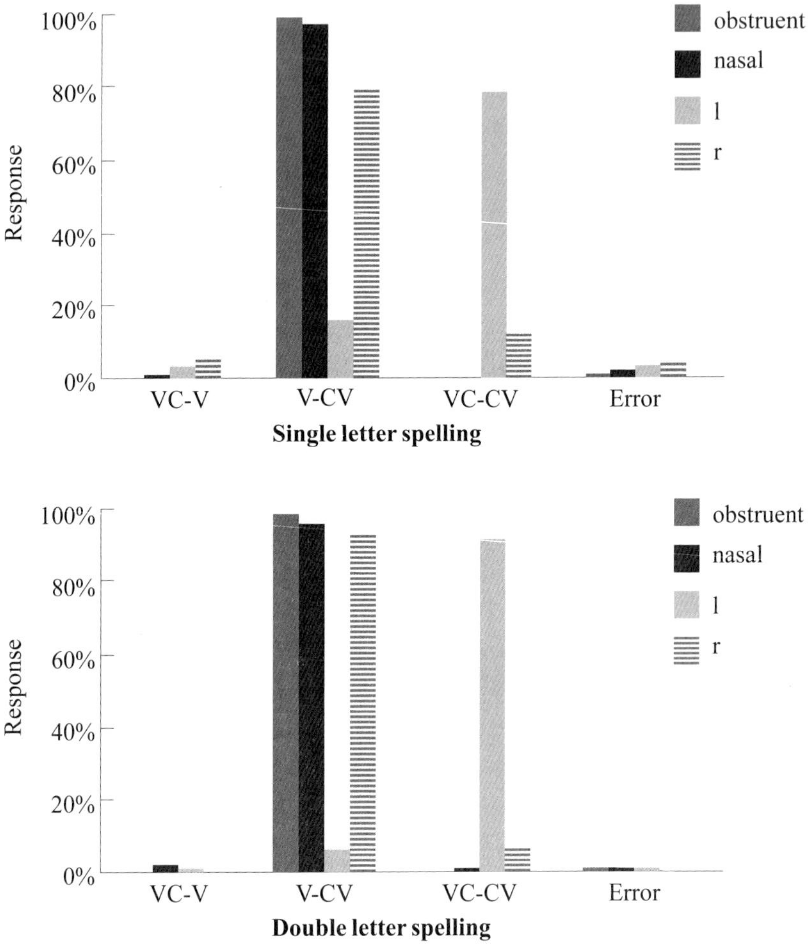

Summary

In Experiment 1, I examined the role of an intervocalic consonant's syllable in bisyllabic English words in an effort to answer to the following questions:

- Is the certain syllabification strategy of Korean, *a strong CV-CV syllabification preference*, also maintained in parsing English words?

- To what extent do the three significant factors manifested by native speakers of English in their English syllabification, *categories of intervocalic consonants, stress placement, and spellings*, affect the Korean speakers' syllabification in English words?

Except for the syllabification of the intervocalic liquids, the strong V-CV syllabification strategy was maintained in syllabification of the English intervocalic consonants by Korean speakers regardless of stress placement and the spellings of the consonants.

The results of this study also show that syllabification of the intervocalic liquids is split into two distinct patterns: 1) The /r/ patterns with other obstruents and nasals showing CV-**C**V syllabification, while 2) the intervocalic /l/ is often syllabified as ambisyllabic as V**C**-**C**V, i.e., the intervocalic /l/ belongs to both the preceding and following syllables at the same time.

Thus far, in Experiment 1, a strikingly higher rate of V-**C**V syllabification pattern was observed except for the syllabification of the intervocalic liquid /l/. This leaves an important issue to be addressed. Is it possible that the strategy used by Korean speakers is just task-driven, and thus, does not reflect general patterns of syllabification by Koreans? Could it be the case that the Korean speakers mainly employed the strategy simply because they found it simple and easy in the syllabification of English words? Or, is it reasonable to further generalize the syllabification patterns of Korean speakers based on results in Experiment 1? In order to answer this, Experiment 2 employed a metalinguistic task, *a syllable reversal task*, e.g., 'demon' → 'mon-de' (Treiman & Danis, 1988; Treiman, 1992; Schiller et al., 1997; Barry et al., 1999; Berg & Niemi, 2000; Berg, 2001; Content et al., 2001; Cebrian, 2002; Bertinetto et al., 2007),[27] which is expected to show general syllabification patterns

27 Developmental evidence indicates that reversal tasks may indeed be harder

by native speakers of Koreans.

Experiment 2

Methods

In their study of English syllabification by native speakers of English, Treiman and Danis (1988) found that there were significant effects of both consonant sonority and spelling on syllabification: The more sonorous the consonants are the more they tend to be ambisyllabified (i.e., as syllabified as V**C**-**C**V) . In addition, they showed that people were more likely to place an intervocalic consonant in both syllables if they thought that the consonant was spelled with a double letter than if they thought that it was spelled with a single letter.

As shown in Experiment 1, however, if we suppress the intervocalic liquid /l/ syllabification responses, the strong V-**C**V syllabification pattern shown by the native speakers of Korean seems to be prevalent regardless of consonant sonority and spelling. By using a more difficult task than Experiment 1, Experiment 2 attempts to confirm whether the observed syllabification pattern, *the V-**C**Vpattern*, is consistent among Korean speakers regardless of the nature of the tasks.

Stimulus Materials

Stimuli for Experiment 2 were 87 monomorphemic bisyllabic English words with a single intervocalic consonant. The stimuli included some words used in Experiment 1 and added some new words which can be categorized as "less frequently used words" (cf. Vitevitch &Luce, 1999; Vitevitch et al., 1999). As in Experiment 1, I varied the intervocalic

---

than other types of metalinguistic tasks (Yopp, 1988). Along the same line, Côté and Kharlamov (2011) point out that "Syllable reversal yields a higher rate of errors than any other task and it is often avoided for this reason, especially with children" (p. 275).

consonants in 1) consonant category (obstruents, nasals, or liquids), 2) stress placement (stressed on the first syllable or on the second syllable) and 3) spelling of intervocalic consonants (with single or double letters) in CVCV environments. The stimuli were, then, randomized, divided into four blocks, and then recorded by the same speaker who recorded the words for Experiment 1. After the recordings were made, each word was separated by approximately 3 seconds of silence using *Cool Edit 2000*.

Participants

The participants (7 males and 14 females) for Experiment 2 were the same those who participated in Experiment 1. As previously mentioned, they were all college students at a university in Seoul, South Korea. And they were all recruited from elective courses at the university, and were paid 10 dollars for their participation. In addition, they were not aware of the purpose of the experiment, nor had they received any explicit phonetic training.

Procedure

As a language game, participants were asked to reverse the two parts of the word they had heard (e.g., 'demon' → mon-de,) through headphones in writing: Specifically, after listening to the recordings through the headphones, the participants were required to write the words starting from the second part of the word using the Korean orthography. For this syllable-reversal task, there was a practice session through which participants familiarized themselves with the task. Since the participants may simply rely on the learned rules of syllabification, the term "syllable" was not employed during the experiment. Instead, participants were instructed to switch the second part over the first part of bisyllabic words.[28] When the participants made a mistake during the

28 Some bisyllabic English words were not perceived as "bisyllabic" by Korean

practice session, the experiment facilitator showed another example along with correct answers to the task instead of correcting the mistakes the participant made. The main experiment session did not proceed until the participant felt comfortable with the task. To minimize the residual effects of the stimuli of Experiment 1, Experiment 2 was carried out one week after Experiment 1.

Experiment 2: Results

Syllabification of English Intervocalic Consonants by Koreans in Syllable Reversal

Figure 2.7. Syllabification of intervocalic consonants by Koreans from syllable reversal tasks (Exp. 2)

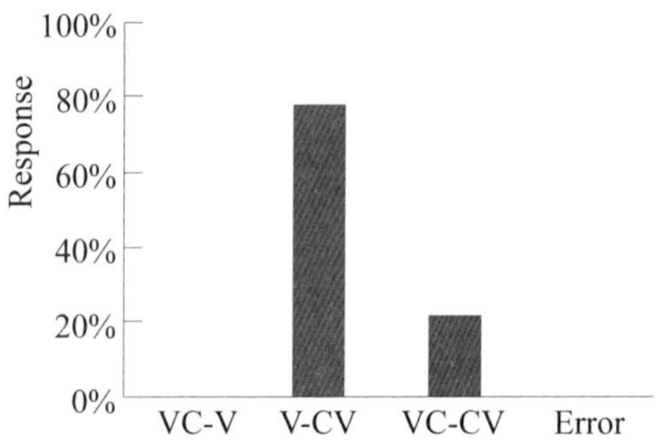

Experiment 2 employed a rather difficult syllable-reversal task in order to see whether the strong syllabification pattern is maintained regardless of the nature of the task employed. Let us first turn to syllabification of intervocalic consonants from the syllable-reversal task in Experiment 2. As shown in Figure 2.7, 78 % of the responses (1417/1827) favor the CV-**C**V syllabification, while 22 % (401/1827) favor ambisyllabic (i.e., CV**C**-**C**V) syllabification. As in Experiment 1, the strong CV-**C**V syllabification is maintained in Experiment 2, suggesting that the CV-**C**V segmentation strategy is

---

listeners. For example, the word 'suffice' can be perceived as a four-syllable word by some Korean listeners. Thus, to counter potential problems in reversing the syllable like this, instructions were also given to start with the second part of the word and end with the first part of the word regardless of how long the words would be. For further discussion of perception of syllables by Korean speakers, see **Chapter 3**.

strong strategy in Korean listeners whether or not the tasks in syllabification vary.

I also examined effects of three factors on syllabification in the following sub-sections: 1) category of the intervocalic consonants, 2) stress placement in words, and 3) spelling of the intervocalic consonants.

Effects of Consonant Category on Syllabification in Syllable Reversal

Table 2.5 shows a cross-tabulation of consonant category against syllabification responses by Korean listeners. Liquids were divided into /l/ and /r/ to examine the difference seen in Experiment 1.

Table 2.5. Cross-tabulations of syllabification and consonant category from syllable reversal tasks (Exp. 2)

consonant category	syllabification				
	VC-V	V-CV	VC-CV	error	total
obstruents		627(99.5%)	2(0.3%)	1(0.2%)	630
nasals	1(0.2%)	587(99.8%)			588
/l/		86(17.8%)	394(81.4%)	4(0.8%)	484
/r/		119(95.2%)	5(4%)	1(0.8%)	125
total	**1(0.1%)**	**1419(77.7%)**	**401(21.9%)**	**6(0.3%)**	**1827**

Obstruents (99%) and nasals (99%) were all syllabified as V-**C**V. Most intervocalic liquid /l/s were syllabified as ambisyllabic as V**C**-**C**V (81%) while almost all intervocalic /r/s (95%) were syllabified as onsets to the following syllables (i.e., V-**C**V). A two-way contingency table analysis using cross-tabs was conducted to find any differences between the observed and expected frequency of each consonant category in its selection of syllabification. There was a significant association between consonant types and selection of syllabification ($x^2 = 1026.93$, df = 6, $p < 0.005$). To evaluate the difference among the portions, multiple pairwise comparisons were conducted. Table 2.6 shows the results of these analyses. Holm's sequential Bonferroni method was used to control

Type 1 error at the .05 level across all comparisons as shown below.

Table 2.6. Results for the pairwise comparison

comparison	Pearson x^2	p-value	significance	Cramer's V
obs-nas	3.87	.275	NS	.056
obs-/l/	794.851	<.0005	*	.845
obs-/r/	17.07	<.0005	*	.150
nas-/l/	769.108	<.0005	*	.847
nas-/r/	28.66	<.0005	*	.200
/l/-/r/	267.79	<.0005	*	.663

(* $p < .008$; NS: non-significant)

The pairwise difference that was significant comes from the comparison against the liquids, which suggests that liquids, especially /l/was a major contributor to the significant x^2 value; that is, liquids, specifically, the liquid /l/ is attributed to more ambisyllabic V**C**-**C**V responses.

Effects of Stress Placement on Syllabification in Syllable Reversal

Stress placement in English words affects the syllabification patterns by Korean listeners when they engaged in syllable reversal tasks. Figure 2.8 shows syllabification of intervocalic consonants as a function of stress placement in English words.

As seen, there were a signficantly higher number of responses for V-**C**V syllabification regardless of stress placement in words: That stress is placed either on the first syllable or the second syllable does not seem to affect the way that Korean listeners parse English words because their preference for the V-CV syllabification was clear and consistent.

As discussed in the previous section, a major contributor to the VC-CV syllabification was the intervocalic /l/, and, thus, it is important to see how stress interacts with each consonant category in terms of syllabification. Table 2.7 shows a cross-tabulation of stress placement against syllabification, separated for each consonant category.

Figure 2.8. Syllabification of intervocalic consonants as a function of stress from syllable reversal tasks (Exp. 2)

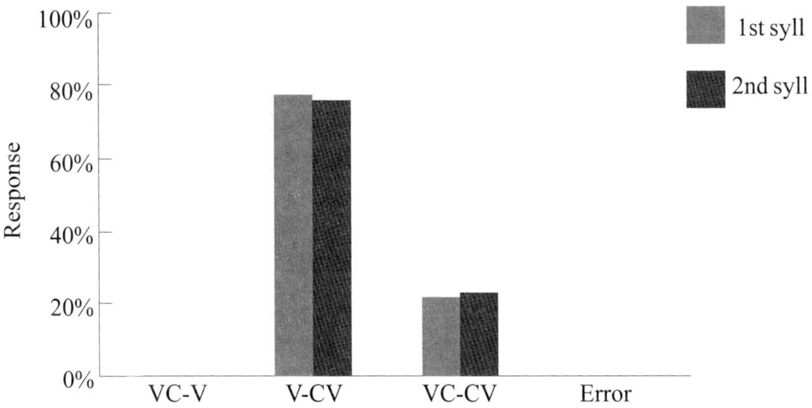

Table 2.7. Cross-tabulation of stress placement against syllabification separated by consonant category

consonant category	stress placement	syllabification				
		VC-V	V-CV	VC-CV	error	total
obstruents	1stsyll		543(99.5%)	2(0.3%)	1(0.1%)	546
	2ndsyll		84(100%)			84
nasals	1stsyll	1(0.2%)	461(99.8%)			462
	2ndsyll		126(100%)			126
/l/	1stsyll		57(15%)	318(84%)	4(1%)	379
	2ndsyll		29(28%)	76(72%)		105
/r/	1stsyll		100(96%)	3(3%)	1(1%)	104
	2ndsyll		19(90%)	2(10%)		21
total		**1(0.1%)**	**1419(77.7%)**	**401(21.9%)**	**6(0.3%)**	**1827**

First, obstruents, nasals, and /r/ show the same pattern in syllabification with the dominant V-**C**V responses independently of stress placement: 1) 99% of the obstruents favor V-**C**V responses when stressed on the first syllable and 100% on the second syllable; 2) as for nasals, 99% and 100% respond to V-**C**V syllabification when stress is placed on the first and second stressed syllables, respectively; 3) finally, 96% and 90% of the intervocalic /r/s were syllabified as V-**C**V when words were stressed on the first syllable and the second syllable, respectively.

Secondly, the ambisyllabic (i.e., V**C**-**C**V) syllabification responses were overwhelming for the intervocalic /l/ regardless of the stress placement in the words. The Chi-Square statistic reveals that there was no significant association between stress placement and syllabification ($x^2 = 1.92$, df = 3, $p = 0.589$). That is, participants consistently assigned the intervocalic consonant to the second syllable (for the intervocalic obstruents, nasals, and the /r/) or to the both syllables (for the intervocalic /l/), independently of the stress placement.

Effects of Spellings on Syllabification in Syllable Reversal

One key issue raised throughout this chapter is the effect of spelling on syllabification. Figure 2.9 shows the effect of spelling on Korean speakers' syllabification in English.

As shown below, the intervocalic obstruents, nasals, and /r/ were all syllabified as an onset to the second syllables (i.e., V-**C**V) independently of whether intervocalic consonants were spelled either with single letter or double letters. However, the intervocalic /l/s also showed a consistency in syllabification in that they were mainly syllabified as ambisyllabic (i.e., V**C**-**C**V) regardless of spelling ($x^2 = 2.043$, df = 3, $p = 0.563$). This suggests that the representation of the intervocalic consonants in orthography, either single or double lettered, does not affect the syllabification process. Or, at least, it appears that the effect of the spelling of the intervocalic consonants on syllabification by native speakers of Korean was not as strong as that reported in Treiman and Danis (1988) in which they examined English speakers' syllabification patterns.

Figure 2.9. Syllabification of intervocalic consonants as a function of spelling from syllable reversal tasks (Exp. 2)

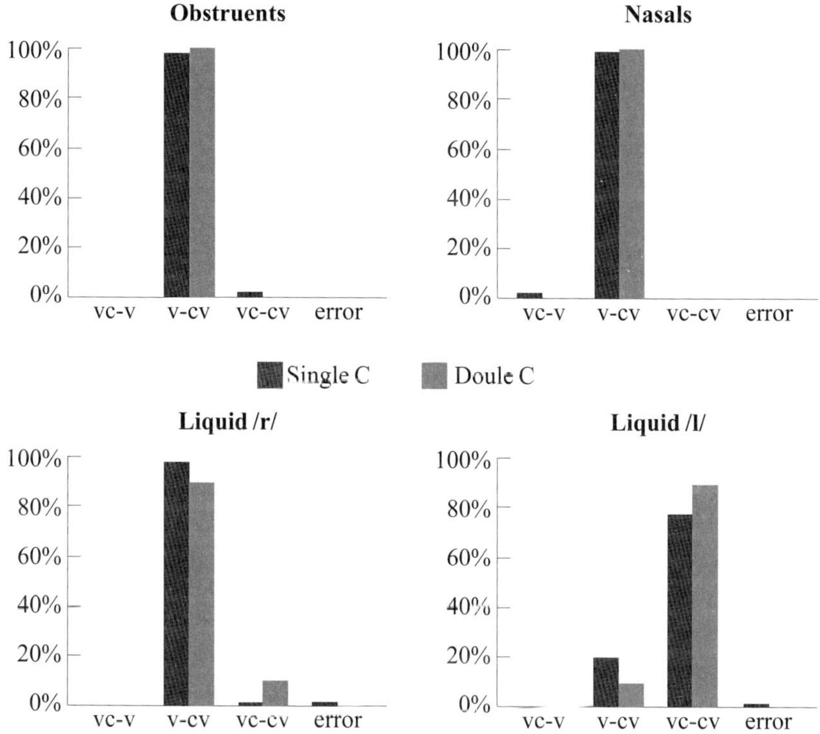

Summary

Experiment 2 confirmed that the strong V-CV syllabification strategy was maintained in English syllabification by Korean speakers even under the circumstances in which the participants might have more difficulty in completing the given task. Here, the participants were asked to reverse the second syllable over the first syllable in English bisyllabic words, which is assumed to be a difficult metalinguistic task (cf. Yopp, 1988).

As shown in Experiment 1, the effects of sonority on syllabification were observed. It was found that only the intervocalic liquids were syllabified as ambisyllabic while the other consonants, *obstruents and nasals*, were all segmented into the second syllable as an onset (i.e., V-C̲V). As for the liquids (/l, r/), a closer examination, however, showed a split in the syllabification since the /l/ alone was the main contributor to this ambisyllabicity (VC̲-C̲V) whereas the /r/ was syllabified as onset to the second syllables (i.e., V-C̲V) as were the other consonants.

There were no effects of stress placement and spelling on syllabification, however. That is, the intervocalic consonants were consistently assigned to the second syllable syllabified as V-CV for obstruents, nasals and the /r/ while ambisyllabically syllabified (VC-CV) for the /l/, independently of the placement of stress in words and of the orthographic representation, *single or double-lettered*, of that consonant.

Discussion

A Strong CV-based Parsing Strategy in English by Koreans

Korean speakers have a consistent strategy of segmenting words with the strings of VCV segments into V-**C**V forms, and it raises the question about whether they do the same when parsing in English? As reported in Treiman and Danis (1988), English syllabification of intervocalic consonants (by native speakers of English) is affected by the phonetic category of the intervocalic consonants, stress placements, and spelling. The results in this chapter, however, show that stress placement and spelling do not influence Korean speakers' parsing of English words. This is probably because they utilize the same strategy for parsing English as they do Korean, which is a CV-structure-based parsing. This CV-based parsing in English by Korean speakers is apparent if we compare Koreans' parsing strategy with that of their English-speaking counterparts. Table 2.8 shows a comparison of the syllabification of intervocalic consonants by Korean speakers (from Experiment 2) with that of English speakers (from Treiman & Danis, 1988). It should be noted, however, that a direct comparison between two studies would be impossible since the two employed different methods of obtaining syllabification patterns for each speaker. But it is still worthwhile to examine the syllabification of intervocalic consonants for the two language groups as in Table 2.8.

Table 2.8. Comparisons of syllabificaton by native speakers of English in Treiman and Danis (1988) vs. native speakers of Korean in Experiment 2

				syllabification by English speakers			**syllabification by Korean speakers**		
				Treiman&Danis(oral task)			Experiment 2		
spell	**stress**	**c-type**	**e.g.**	**VC-V**	**V-CV**	**VC-CV**	**VC-V**	**V-CV**	**VC-CV**
1	1	L	melon	47%%	30%	23%	0%	32%	66%
1	1	N	lemon	50%	2%	17%	0.3%	99%	0%
1	1	O	seven	35%	49%	16%	0%	99%	0.4%
1	2	L	relate	12%	78%	10%	0%	37%	63%
1	2	N	canoe	8%	84%	8%	0%	100%	0%
1	2	O	guitar	6%	93%	1%	0%	100%	0%
2	1	L	borrow	13%	8%	78%	0%	33%	67%
2	1	N	bonnet	14%	6%	80%	0%	100%	0%
2	1	O	bobbin	14%	11%	75%	0%	100%	0%
2	2	L	balloon	6%	35%	59%	0%	39%	61%
2	2	N	connect	7%	29%	64%	0%	100%	0%
2	2	O	buffet	6%	47%	48%	0%	100%	0%

(L: liquid; N: nasal; O: obstruent)

Treiman and Danis (1988) found that sonority is one major factor in ambisyllabification: The more sonorous intervocalic consonants are, the more likely they are to be syllabified as ambisyllabic (VC-CV). Another factor to consider is an effect of spelling on syllabification. Treiman and Danis (1988) reported that English speakers were more likely to place an intervocalic consonant into both preceding and following syllables if they thought that the consonant was spelled with a double letter than if they thought it was spelled with a single letter.

They suggest that double-letter spelling may promote ambisyllabicity of intervocalic consonants. On the other hand, the syllabification of intervocalic consonants by Korean speakers overwhelmingly belongs to the second syllable as an onset, i.e., V-C̲V, except with /l/. This strong (V-)CV-based parsing was consistent regardless of stress placement and spelling. Furthermore, CV syllable structure seems to be the most frequent in Korean (cf. S-C. Ahn, 1998), and thus it is possible to posit that the CV is the predominant syllable type used by native speakers of Korean in their parsing of Korean as well as English.

The Status of Liquids in Korean Phonology: Ambisyllabic or Geminates?

Results show that the intervocalic /l/ stands out in that it shows a consistent syllabification pattern, VC-CV syllabification, which is quite different from those of other consonants, regardless of stress-placement or spelling. An important issue to address, then, is why it is only the lateral /l/, not the /r/, that shows this VC-CV syllabification. Two possible answers would be because of intervocalic liquid ambisyllabic in Korean (Kang, 1991; Smith, 1997) or the geminate status of intervocalic liquid in Korean (Kang, 1991)? Before addressing the issue, it is necessary to clarify the difference between two terms, *ambisyllabicity* and *gemination.*[29] In her dissertation on intervocalic consonants in Lheidli,[30] Bird (2002) nicely clarifies the difference between the two terms:

> By and large, *ambisyllabicity* is used in reference to syllabification in stress-timed languages. For example, the [m] in *lemon* is perceived as belonging to both syllables of the word: [lɛm.mən]. *Gemination*, on the other hand, is used in languages such as Japanese, Italian, or Turkish which contrast long and short consonants. (p.281)

---

29 For what is said about ambisyllabicity and gemination in the literature, see Bird (2002).

30 Lheidli is a dialect of Dakelh (Carrier) spoken in the Prince George area, British Columbia, Canada (Bird, 2002).

She summarizes the differences between ambisyllabicity and gemination as follows.

Table 2.9. Ambisyllabicity vs. gemination(adapted from Bird, 2002, p. 283)

ambisyllabicity	gemination
• consonants are usually short (e.g. flaps)	• consonants are usually long
• not moraic	• moraic
• driven by prosody[31]	• not driven by prosody
• not contrastive	• contrastive (long vs. short)

The difference is also captured in the formal representations of ambisyllabic consonants and geminates[32] as shown in (4).

(4) Formal representations of ambisyllabic and geminate consonants (from Bird, 2002: 285-286)

a. Hayes' (1989) representation

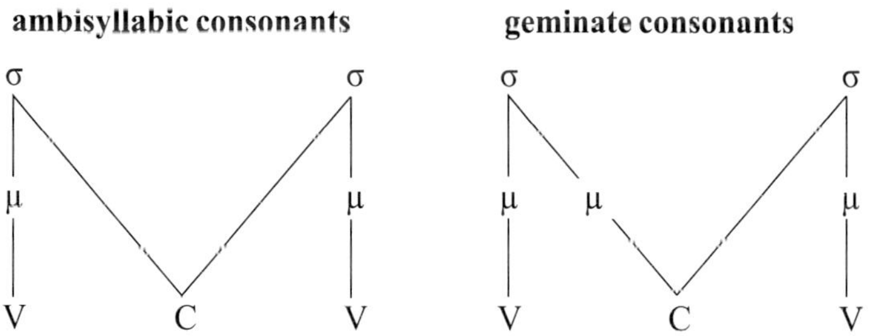

b. Hume et al. (1997a, 1997b)'s representation

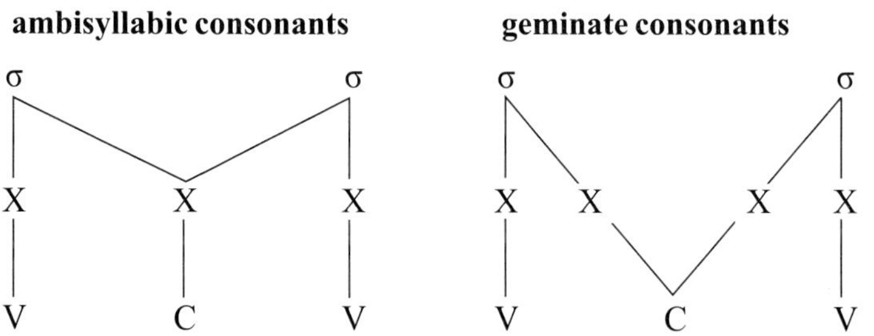

31 For example, prosody ensures that stressed syllables are closed.

According to Hayes (1989), geminate consonants are underlyingly associated with morae, and thus, they are distinguished from ambisyllabic consonants in the formal representation as shown in (4a). Disagreeing with Hayes's moraic approach, which argues that geminates are always moraic, Hume et al., (1997a, 1997b) argue that geminates are not necessarily moraic based on non-moraic word-initial geminates in Leti. Rather, they differentiate ambisyllabic consonants from geminates by the number of X-slots associated with them: Ambisyllabic consonants are associated with only one X-slot while geminate consonants are associated with two X-slots as shown in (4b).

Having clarified the difference between ambisyllabicity and gemination, I now move on to the liquid in Korean. Korean has only one liquid in the phoneme inventory, which is underlyingly represented as /L/[33] with different alternations on the surface depending on which syllable position the liquid would occur in as in (5).

(5) Liquid alternations in Korean

a. Onset position: /L/ → [n]
/Lakwon/ → [nak.won] 'paradise'
/Loin/ → [no.in] 'old man'

---

32 "Borowsky et al. (1984) claim that ambisyllabicity and gemination are descriptive terms used in reference to different phenomena, but that these two terms refer to the same formal structure. They argue that the phonetic differences between ambisyllabic and geminate consonants stem from their phonological role. Consonants which are specified underlyingly as belonging to both syllables are implemented phonetically as geminates. Consonants which become part of both syllables as a result of prosodic requirements are implemented phonetically as ambisyllabic –"as in the flap in the American English pronunciation of city" (as cited in Bird, 2002, p. 284).

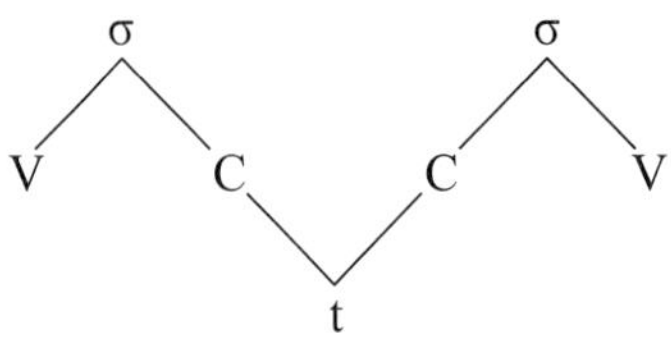

(Borowsky et al. (1984) representation of geminate and ambisyllabic consonants).

33 Here, I use an archiphonemic representation /L/ for the underlying representation of the liquid in Korean. Depending on the scholar, however, either /l/ or /r/ can be chosen for the underlying representation of the liquids in Korean.

b. Coda position: /L/ → [l]
/muL/ → [mul] 'water'
/KaLta/ → [kal.da] 'to change, exchange'

c. Intervocalic position: /L/ → [ɾ]
/paLam/ → [pa.ɾam] 'wind'
/taLi/ → [ta.ɾi] 'leg'

(Note: The dot indicates a syllable boundary; the phonetic forms in the square brackets represent spoken forms)

As shown in (5a) and (5b), the /L/ is pronounced as [n] in word (or syllable-) initial position while it is pronounced as [l] in syllable final position. Interestingly, the /L/ is realized as [ɾ] intervocalically as in (5c). Based on these alternations, Kang (1991) argues that the intervocalic [ɾ] should be interpreted as an ambisyllabic segment because it is neither the onset of the second syllable nor the coda of the first syllable.

In Korean, there exist both ambisyllabic and geminate consonants as shown in (6).

(6) Geminates [ll] vs. singleton [ɾ] in intervocalic position (adapted Lee, 2001)

a. [mollæ] 'secretly' 몰래 vs. [moɾæ] 'sand' 모래
b. [mulli] 'physics' 물리 vs. [muɾi] 'group' 무리
c. [əllita] 'freeze' 얼리다 vs. [əɾita] 'be young' 어리다

The informatioin in (6) shows that the geminate [ll] and the singleton [ɾ] are contrastive in intervocalic position. These liquid alternations are summarized in Table 2.10 .

Table 2.10. Liquid alternations in Korean

Korean liquid /L/	surface realizations		
	in onset position	in coda position	intervocalic position
	[n]	[l]	[ll]: geminates [ɾ]: ambisyllabic

Let us return to the question of why the English intervocalic /l/s are generally syllabified as VC-CV while the other intervocalic obstruents, nasals, and /r/s are syllabified as V-CV by native speakers of Korean. It seems that the VC-CV syllabification employed by Koreans for the English intervocalic /l/s stems from the status of the intervocalic geminate [ll] in Korean, which is shown in Table 2.10.

We also see the effects of the Korean intervocalic [ɾ] on the syllabification of the English words. Based on the distribution of the liquid in Korean, Lee (2001) proposes a moraic approach to the English /l/ adaptation in Korean loanwords in which lateral [l] is licensed in moraic position and flap [ɾ] appears in non-moraic positions. Her proposal is based on an assumption that geminates are moraic (Hayes, 1989; Davis, 1999),[34] and that Korean codas are moraic[35] according to Jun (1993, 1994). Assuming the geminate status of intervocalic /l/, she showed variations of English intervocalic /l/ adaptation in Korean loanwords as shown in (7).

(7) Variations of intervocalic [l] adaptation in loanwords (adapted from Lee, 2001)

English	Variations in Korean orthographic adaptation	
	Variation I	**Variation II**
a. kilo	[kʰil.lo]	[kʰi.ɾo]
b. jelly	[cel.li]	[ce.ɾi]
c. melon	[mel.lon]	[me.ɾon]
d. blouse	[pul.la.u.sɨ]	[pu.ɾa.u.sɨ]
e. chocolate	[cʰo.kʰol.let]	[cʰo.kʰo.ɾet]
f. ambulance	[am.bul.lan.sɨ]	[am.bu.ɾan.sɨ]

As shown in (7), the adaptation of the English intervocalic /l/ varies either as geminate [ll] as shown in column (I) or as singleton [ɾ] as in column (II).[36]

---

34 For non-moraic geminate analyses, see Tranel (1991), Hume et al. (1997a, 1997b).

35 For an argument of non-moraic status of codas in Korean, see Tak (1997).

36 Lee (2001) argued that given the same input, the forms in column (I) result from

This variation of the intervocalic English /l/ is also found in Korean orthography. In Korean orthography, the representation of allophones of /L/- i.e., intervocalic [ɾ] or syllable-final [l] - is expressed with the same symbol 'ㄹ'. Thus, when it comes to the orthographic representation of loanwords from English where the distinction between [l] and [ɾ] is phonemic, the phonemic distinction between English /l/ and /r/ is neutralized in Korean orthography as shown in the column of Korean orthographic representation in (8).

(8) Korean orthography of English /l/ and /r/

English			**Korean orthographic representation**
a. Syllable-initially			
radio	→	[**r**a.di.o]	라디오
lion	→	[**r**a.i.on]	라이온
b. Syllable-finally			
car	→	[k^{h}a]	카
call	→	[k^{h}o**l**]	콜
c. Intervocalically			
caramel	→	[k^{h}a.**ɾ**a.mel]	카라멜
cola	→	[k^{h}o**l.l**a]	콜라
d. Pre-consonantally			
skirt	→	[su.k^{h}ə.t^{h}ɨ]	스커트
cult	→	[k^{h}əl.t^{h}ɨ]	컬트

As shown in (8a), syllable initial English /l/ and /r/ are represented by the same symbol in Korean orthography, which is well matched to the fact that Korean has only liquid /L/ in its phoneme inventory. Korean orthography well represents the complementary distribution

---

the loanword constraint ranking while the forms in column (II) from the native constraint ranking. Supporting the core-periphery organization of the lexicon (Ito & Mester, 1995), she proposes stratification of loanwords by which variation within loanwords is explained by co-existing rankings: Less nativized items strictly follow the loanword ranking, while more nativized ones are sometimes subject to the native ranking.

of allophones [l] and [ɾ] in that the syllable final /r/ in English words is not expressed at all while the syllable final /l/ is in its orthography represented as 'ㄹ' as shown in (8b) and (8d), respectively. When it comes to the intervocalic /l/ and /r/ in English, the Korean orthography expresses the difference between the two by using a double letter 'ㄹ' for the intervocalic /l/ (as 'ㄹㄹ') and with a single 'ㄹ' for the intervocalic English /r/ as shown in (8c).

However, as pointed out in (7), the English intervocalic /l/ has variations in the Korean orthographic representation as well as its spoken forms as in (9).

(9) Variation of intervocalic English /l/ in spoken and orthographic representations in Korean (adapted from Lee, 2001)

English	Korean			
	(I) Korean-orthography 1		**(II)Korean-orthography 2**	
kilo	[kʰil.lo]	킬로	[kʰi.ɾo]	키로
jelly	[cel.li]	젤리	[ce.ɾi]	제리
melon	[mel.lon]	멜론	[me.ɾon]	메론
blouse	[pul.la.u.sɨ]	블라우스	[pu.ɾa.u.sɨ]	브라우스

Therefore, there seem to be two strategies for representing English intervocalic /l/s in the Korean orthographic representations. One strategy is that, in order to keep more English-like pronunciation /l/ (and follow the intervocalic geminate [ll] in Korean), Korean orthography doubles the 'ㄹ' over syllable boundary resulting in a geminate ('-ll-') 'ㄹㄹ' in words. The other strategy is to resort to the strategy of intervocalic [ɾ] in Korean with a single 'ㄹ' at the expense of the English-like pronunciation of /l/. These two strategies seem to be in competition resulting in two different variations of orthographic representations in Korean as shown in (9). In some cases, one strategy wins over the other such that specific orthographic representations would emerge on the surface phonetic forms as pronunciation (e.g., [kʰil.lo] 킬로vs. [kʰi.ɾo] 키로 for 'kilo'). In relation to this, Chapter 3 will look into these strategies further in terms of ranking and competition.

Self-Evaluation of Their English Proficiency by Koreans

As shown in the results of their English skills in four areas (reading, writing, listening, and speaking), the Korean participants who participated in the experiments seemed to be quite conservative in their ratings. Although it was not my main concern to rate their English proficiency for the purpose of the current study, it is worth mentioning the participants' self-evaluations of their English proficiency in this study. Extremely low-rated Korean participants' self-rating on their English proficiency may come from their "humble attitudes," which probably reflect their cultural characteristics (cf. Gardener, 1979).In relation to the Korean college students' attitudes toward their English proficiency, this is probably because of the way Koreans, in general, have such high expectations of themselves, especially in regards to academic performance, and thus they were probably not satisfied with their English abilities. This could be translated into the fact that Korean learners of English tend to underrate their own proficiency in English (cf. Lim, 2003), and this may also be illustrated in the current findings.

Summary

In this chapter, it was shown that the parsing strategies, the strongly CV-based syllabification, in a native language (L1: Korean), were employed even in the syllabification of the target language (L2: English). In addition, other questions emerging from this inquiry were: "To what extent do the three significant factors in English syllabification, 1) category of intervocalic consonants, 2) stress placement, and 3) spellings, affect the Korean speakers' syllabification in bisyllabic English words?" An effect of sonority of intervocalic consonants was observed in that the intervocalic /l/s are syllabified as VC-CV while the other intervocalic consonants, obstruents, nasals, and /r/s, were all syllabified with the following syllable as an onset, i.e., V-CV, independently of the stress placement and the spelling of those consonants by Korean listeners. In relation to this, it is possible that the VC-CV syllabification of the intervocalic English /l/s by native speakers of Koreans stem from the "special" status of the intervocalic liquid /L/ as geminate [ll] in Korean phonology.

CHAPTER 3

SEGMENTATION AND SYLLABLE COUNTING

Introduction

In the previous chapter, the native speakers of Korean who participated in the experiment seem unaffected by differences in stress placement and spelling when parsing English words, because, it appears that they utilize the strategy of CV-structure-based parsing as they do when parsing native Korean words. Given the difference in what constitutes a syllable unit in Korean and English, along with this CV-based syllabification manifested by Koreans, Korean speakers may have difficulty perceiving syllables as single units in English words. In addition, with a hypothesis in which "rhythm is considered a central organizing factor in speech perception and production," Erickson, Akahane-Yamada, Tajima and Matsumoto (1999) suggest that L1 rhythmic units may interfere with the perception of L2 rhythmic units.

Languages may differ in the degree to which syllable boundaries are clear and unambiguous. According to Cutler, Mehler, Norris and Segui (1986, p. 397) "stress languages tend to have greater variation in syllable weight than non-stress languages, and partly as a consequence of stress assignment, syllable boundaries in stress languages are frequently unclear." Consequently, English speakers may vary in how they devide internally depending on stress placement, segmental make-up and the phonetic nature of vowels within words (Treiman & Danis, 1988). Even though syllable boundaries in English are not clear, determining the number of syllables contained in a given English word or utterance, is not usually controversial. This difference between syllable counts and syllable boundaries was pointed out earlier by Abercrombie (1967, p. 34): "Most people seem to be able to say, without much difficulty, how many syllables are contained in a word or utterance; and with perhaps somewhat more difficulty, to say where each syllable begins and ends…". Erickson et al. (1999)[37] also showed that English speakers seem to be well aware of how many syllables are contained in a given English word or utterance.

Interestingly, many observations show that Korean speakers do not display this same ambiguous understanding of syllable divisions of English words. However, they inconsistently count the number of syllables in English words (cf. Lim, 2003). Thus, in relation to syllable boundary and syllable counts, the current chapter further investigates, 1) whether native speakers of Korean may perceive syllables in English words, and if so, compared to native speakers of English, how differently they would count syllables of the words, and 2) what factors may contribute to Koreans' perception of syllables in terms of syllable boundary and syllable counting. In so doing, I will closely look at two typologically different languages, *English*, stress-based language and *Korean*, syllable-based language. For L2 learner perspectives, I will examine how Korean learners of English perceive English words in terms of syllable counts and syllable boundary.

Syllable Counts of English Words by Koreans

The following sections examine the syllable counts made by Koreans of English words from Korean orthographic representation of the English words. The motivation for choosing to use Korean in this study is two-fold. First, Korean is transparent in terms of mapping sounds onto letters such that the relationship between spoken and written representations of speech is relatively straightforward and the representations are faith-

37 Erickson et al. (1999) conducted a syllable counting experiment with a set of 275 English words varying in number of syllables, consonants, and vowels. Native English listeners correctly identified the numbers of syllables in the English words approximately 98% of the time, whereas Japanese listeners correctly identified the number of syllables 57% of the time.

ful to one another.[38] Second, the Korean orthographic representation is visually syllable-based; each syllable should be expressed within a virtual syllabic block. Therefore, the orthography, itself, reveals clear syllable divisions within words, easily allowing for straightforward syllable counts.

Observations of Syllable Counts by Koreans

In this section, I provide some observations of syllable counts made by Koreans of English words from Korean orthographic representation of the English words. Example (1) shows some examples of syllable counts of monosyllabic English words by Koreans.

(1) Syllable counts of English words by Koreans (All the examples come from the guidelines for representing English loanwords in Korean by the Ministry of Education, 1986, 1992: see Appendix B)

mono-syllabic English words	**syllable counts by Koreans**
gap	갭[kap¬] (1)
book	북[puk¬] (1)
kid	키드 [k^{h}i.dɨ] (2)
jazz	재즈[dʒæ.dʒɨ] (2)
land	랜드[ɾœn.dɨ] (2)
act	액트 [æk.t^{h}ɨ] (2)
corn	콘 [k^{h}on] (1)
team	팀 [t^{h}im] (1)
wool	울 [wul] (1)
make	메이크 [me.i.khɨ] (3)
stamp	스탬프 [sɨ.t^{h}æm.p^{h}ɨ] (3)

(Numbers in parentheses are syllable counts by Koreans, and dots indicate syllable boundaries. In addition, 'C¬' indicates an unreleased stop word-finally.)

38 For detailed descriptions on Koran orthography, see Chapter 1. The interplay between perception and orthography will be pursued in detail in Chapter 6.

As shown in (1), syllable counts by native speakers of Korean of monosyllabic English words seem to vary. In relation to this, several points are noticed. First, a voiced word-final stop seems to contribute to counting the monosyllabic word as two syllables (e.g., the word 'kid' was counted as two syllables (키드 [k^{h}i.dɨ]) while 'gap' is counted as one syllable as 갭[kap˺]). Second, when there are word-initial or word-final consonant clusters, Korean speakers usually add extra syllables by adding vowel epenthesis (e.g., 'stamp' counted as three syllables as 스탬프 [sɨ.t^{h}æm.p^{h}ɨ]). Interestingly, English long vowels, however, do not seem to contribute to syllable counts (e.g., long vowels in 'team' and 'wool' are both counted as one syllable), whereas diphthongs are counted as more than one syllable (e.g., 'make' counted as three syllables as shown in 메이크 [me.i.k^{h}ɨ]).

Experiment

Given the inconsistent syllable counting of English words made by Koreans, in the following experiment, I aim to further investigate how Koreans count syllables of English words by varying stress placement, final segments, and vowel quality.

Methods

Regarding the relationship between syllable boundary and syllable count by language users, the current experiment investigates whether Koreans have difficulty perceiving syllables in English words, and what factors contribute to Koreans' perception of syllables. In so doing, I examine the way native speakers of Korean count syllables in bisyllabic English words which vary stress placement and final segments. I also examine the effects of final vowel quality on syllable counts by Koreans.

Participants

Twenty-one (7 male and 14 female) native speakers of Standard Korean took part in the experiment.[39] They were all students at a South Korean university in Seoul, Korea, with no self-reported speech or hearing disorders. They were paid for their participation.

Materials

The experiment used 141 mono-morphemic bisyllabic English words selected from Treiman and Danis (1988) with variations of 1) stress-placement (first vs. second syllables), 2) word-final segments (stops vs. nasals vs. liquids vs. vowels), and 3) vowel quality of final vowels in words (lax vs. tense vs. diphthong) as shown in (2) and (3).

(2) Some example words with various final segments

final segment	**stress on the 1st syllable**	**stress on the 2nd syllable**
stop	rabbit	depend
nasal	melon	balloon
liquid	camel	reveal

(3) Some example words with various final vowels

final segment	**stress on the 1st syllable**	**stress on the 2nd syllable**
lax	comma	??? (N/A)
tense	lobby	canoe
diphthong	Judo	deny

All stimulus materials were recorded in a clear-speech-style by a male native speaker of American English from Michigan. The stimuli were randomized, divided into four blocks, and recorded with a Sony microphone directly to digital files in the recording-room of the Linguistics Department at Indiana University. The stimuli were separated by approximately three seconds of silence using the speech editing software *Cool Edit 2000*.

39 For detailed descriptions of the participants, see Chatper 2.

Procedure

Participants were asked to write down each English word they had just heard through headphones using Korean orthography. As mentioned, Korean orthography shows clear boundaries between morphemes since each vowel and consonant are combined such that each morpheme fits into a syllable-based unit. Therefore, it is expected that this written task will show a syllabification process of English by Koreans, from which we can count syllable numbers. The participants showed no difficulty with the task in a warm-up session of five sample words. The order of presentation of the four blocks was randomized for each participant. The experiment was conducted individually to 21 participants using a personal laptop computer in a quiet room.

Results

Relationship Between Stress Placement and Syllable Counts

Figure 3.1. Syllable count by Koreans of bisyallbic English words with varying stress-placement

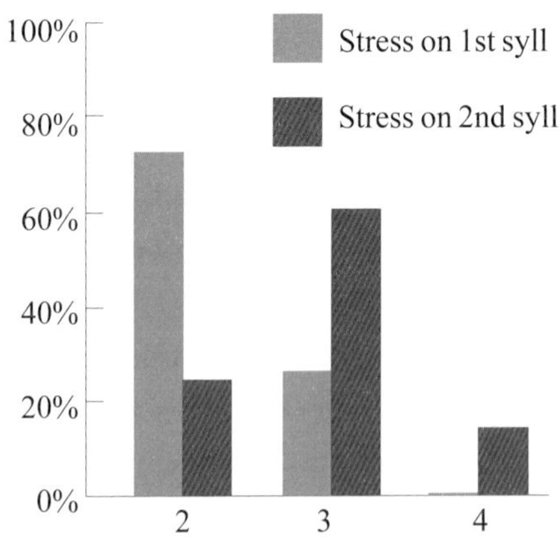

The results were analyzed based on a total of 2961 responses (141 words * 21 participants). Figure 3.1 displays the syllable counts by Koreans from bisyllabic English words with varying stress-placement (i.e., stress is placed either on the first syllable or the second syllable). As shown, the Korean participants were inconsistent in their counts of bisyllabic English words. To be more specific, for 141 bisyllabic English words, 58% (1712/2961) of the total responses by Koreans were counted as bisyllabic, and 37% (1102/2961) as trisyllablic. There were even a few responses as four-syllables (5%: 147/2961).

In this study when words have first syllable stress, they are perceived differently from words with second syllable stress ($x^2(2) = 802.876$, $p < 0.001$). That is, when words have a stress on the first syllable there are proportionally more responses as bisyllabic (62%: 1492/2394) than when words have a stress on the second syllable (19%: 228/1197). Interestingly, when the stress is placed on the second syllable, 81% (969/1197) of the responses count the bisyllabic English words as having three or more syllables.

In the following section, I will investigate in detail how different final segments (i.e., stop, nasal, liquid, or vowel) would affect syllable counts by native speakers of Korean of bisyllabic English words.

Effects of Final Segments on Syllable Counts

Table 3.1 provides the detailed statistics of the Korean participants' syllable counts of the bisyllabic English words according to the category of the word final segment: stop, nasal, liquid, or vowel.

Table 3.1. The Korean participants' syllable counts of bisyllabic English words with varying phonetic nature of the final segments

		phonetic nature of final segment			
stress on	syllable count	stop	nasal	liquid	vowel
1st syllable	2	60.3%(342/567)	83.2%(332/399)	81.6%(377/462)	71.1%(433/609)
	3	39%(221/567)	16.3% (65/399)	18% (83/462)	28.1%(171/609)
	4	0.7% (4/567)	0.5% (2/399)	0.4% (2/462)	0.8% (5/609)
2nd syllable	2	1.9% (8/420)	68.6% (72/105)	57.7%(109/189)	18.6% (39/210)
	3	73.8%(310/420)	24.8% (26/105)	30.2%(57/189)	80.5%(169/210)
	4	24.3%(102/420)	6.7% (7/105)	12.2%(23/189)	1% (2/210)

There are several things to be noticed about how the word final segments influence syllable counts. First, when the first syllable is stressed, words ending with a nasal or liquid are counted as bisyllabic more than 80 percent of the time, while the words ending in a stop are considered bisyllabic only 60% of the time. Instead, words ending in a stop were counted as three syllables or more at a rate 40 %, which is proportionally much higher than words ending in either a nasal (17%) or liquid (18%). The proportion of syllable counts as more than bisyllabic becomes even bigger when the words are stressed on the second syllable as shown in the bottom half of the third column in Table 3.1. As shown, almost 98 percent of bisyllabic English words that ended in a stop and had second syllable stress were counted as having more than three syllables.

Secondly, unlike the stop-final words, the words ending with a nasal or liquid show a higher proportion of bisyllabic counts regardless of stress-placement, even if this tendency becomes weaker when stress is placed on the second syllable rather than the first, as shown in the forth and fifth columns respectively.

Finally, when words end in a vowel and are stressed on the second syllable, more than 80 percent of the responses were counted as having three syllables, as shown in the bottom of the last column.

I have thus far shown that the native speakers of Korean tend to assign bisyllabic English words a syllable count of more than two when the words end in a stop while they tend to count words ending in a nasal or liquid as bisyllabic. This tendency to add to the syllable counts of words ending with a stop could be due to the addition of a vowel to the syllable final stops. As suggested in Lim, Nagao and de Jong (2003), syllable-final neutralization in Korean[40] would probably make it difficult for Koreans to perceive English voicing contrasts in the syllable final position. Furthermore, this neutralization phenomenon could pos-

40 Korean has a three-way contrast in stops syllable-initially, – e.g., lax stops /p, t, k/, tense stops /p', t', k'/, and aspirated stops /p^h, t^h, k^h/ and this three-way contrast is neutralized into lax stops in syllable final (or coda) positions (Martin, 1951; Lee, 1972, Kim-Renaud, 1974; C.W. Kim, 1979; Chung, 1980). For detailed descriptions of syllable-final neutralization, or coda-neutralization, in Korean, see Chapter 6.

sibly bias Korean listeners to perceive syllable final stops as unreleased because Korean stops in syllable-final position are usually produced as unreleased.[41] Given this tendency, if Koreans hear a word-final released stop, they may hear this stop as being in the syllable initial position rather than in the final position, which might affect the syllable count. This possibility is further explored through examining whether the participants viewed the word final stops were released or unreleased. I examined the status of stop releases at the end of the words produced by a Midwestern American speaker in the experiment as in Table 3.2.

Table 3.2. Production of stop releases by a Midwestern American speaker

stress	final stops released	final stops unreleased
1st syllable	63% (17/27)	37% (10/27)
2nd syllable	95% (19/20)	5% (1/20)

In the recording that the participants heard, the Midwestern American speaker produced released or unreleased word-final stops, while he almost always released the final stops for the words with stress on the second syllable. In order to see whether or not the word-final stop release affects syllable counts, I re-tabulated the Koreans' syllable counts of bisyllabic words ending with a stop separating the status of stop release

41 Definitions of 'released/unreleased' can vary. According to Selkirk (1982, p. 373), "a consonant is released if immediately following the articulation and not during or after the articulation of a following segment, the closure is reopened". Henderson and Repp (1982, p. 80) define in this way; "A stop is unreleased if the occlusion is maintained, as in a stop preceding a homorganic stop or in many utterance-final stops with delayed release". Based on auditory perception, Steriade (1993, p. 403) defines a stop release as "an audible release, audible either because accompanied by burst or because it is released with audible friction." For Korean obstruents, Kim-Renaud (1974, p.111) defines unreleased as "completely closing the air passage". Based on acoustic data in English and Korean coda stops, H. Kim (1998) proposes "a released stop is associated with a pulmonic egressive airstream, acoustically manifested as a sharp rise in the energy curve, followed by a high energy plateau after oral burst. An released stop is realized either as the absence of an oral burst with no pulmonic egressive airstream or as a low-amplitude burst involving an ingressive air stream" (pp.365-366). Based on this new definition of 'release/unrelease', "Korean coda consonants are always unreleased while English coda consonants are either released or unreleased" (p.366).

as shown in Table 3.3.

Table 3.3. Syllable counts of bisyllabic words ending in a stop

stress	syllable count	stops combined	released stops	unreleased stops
1st syllable	2	60.3%(342/567)	64.7%(237/357)	52.9%(111/210)
	3	39%(221/567)	34.5%(123/357)	46.7% (98/210)
	4	0.7% (4/567)	0.8% (3/357)	0.5% (1/210)
2nd syllable	2	1.9% (8/420)	1.5% (6/399)	9.5% (2/21)
	3	73.8%(310/420)	72.9%(291/399)	90.5% (19/21)
	4	24.3%(102/420)	25.6%(102/399)	0% (0/21)

Table 3.3 shows that there was a significant association between syllable count and stop release ($x^2(2) = 8.386$, $p = 0.015$ for stress on the first syllable; $x^2(2) = 12.937$, $p = 0.002$ for stress on the second syllable). Especially, when words are stressed on the second syllable, where word-final stops are almost always released as seen in Table 3.3, 98% of the responses counted them as having more than 2 syllables, as shown in the bottom half of the fourth column. However, as the table also shows, bisyllabic words are considered to have more than two even if the word-final stops are not released as shown in the bottom half of the fifth column. This suggests that the presence (or absence) of a stop release at the end of a word alone may not necessarily account for the additional syllable counts. Rather, placement of stress (i.e., on the second syllable over the first syllable) may weigh more in terms of syllable counts by Koreans.

Vowel Quality and Syllable Counts

Finally, I turn to the effects of final-vowel quality on syllable counts. Table 3.4 contains syllable counts of bisyllabic words ending in various vowels: 1) lax, 2) tense, and 3) diphthong.

Table 3.4. Effects of final vowel quality on syllable counts

			final vowel quality		
stress on	**syll_ count**	**vowels combined**	**lax**	**tense**	**diphthong**
1st syllable	2	71.1%(433/609)	93.7%(59/63)	79.9%(302/378)	42.9% (72/168)
	3	28.1%(171/609)	6.3% (4/63)	18.8% (71/378)	57.1% (96/168)
	4	0.8% (5/609)	0% (0/63)	1.3% (5/378)	0% (0/168)
2nd syllable	2	18.6% (39/210)	N/A	76.2% (32/42)	4.2% (7/168)
	3	80.5%(169/210)	N/A	23.8% (10/42)	94.6%(159/168)
	4	1% (2/210)	N/A	0% (0/42)	1.2% (2/168)

There was a significant association between syllable count and final-vowel quality ($x^2(4)=103.288, p<0.001$ for stress on the first syllable; $x^2(2)=115.301, p=<0.001$ for stress on the second syllable). Compared to words ending in either lax or tense vowels, there are proportionally more responses of three syllables or more when words end in diphthongal vowels. This proportion becomes even bigger when the words are stressed on the second syllable as shown in the last column in Table 3.4.

Discussion

In Chapter 3, I have shown that words with stress on the first syllables are different from words stressed on the second syllables in terms of syllable count made by Koreans. Specifically, when it comes to syllable counting by Korean speakers of bisyllabic English words, there are proportionally more responses counting the bisyllabic words as they were when the first syllable is stressed than the second syllable is stressed.

It also shows that these participants count word-final stops differently than word-final nasals and liquids. That is, bisyllabic English words with final stops often tend to be counted as having more than two syllables while words ending with a nasal or liquid are generally counted as bisyllabic. These results agree with a previous finding that "sonorants are more closely linked to a preceding vowel than are obstruents" (Treiman & Danis, 1988, p. 100). Regarding syllable counting by Koreans, there seems to be a tendency to add additional syllables to the syllable counts of words, especially to words ending with a stop, and this tendency could be due to the addition of a vowel (i.e., by way of vowel epenthesis) to the syllable final stops. For perceptual epenthesis, Dupoux, Kahehi, Hirose, Pallier, and Mehler (1999) suggest that the Japanese listeners tend to perceive epenthentic vowels within ill-formed consonantal sequences, which violates the phonotactics in Japanese. Replicating Dupoux et al., (1999), in a perception study of word-medial English consonantal sequences (e.g., VC1.C2V) by Korean speakers, Kabak and Idsardi (2007) confirm that perceptual epenthesis in a second language (L2, *English*) arises from syllable structure restrcictions of the first language (L1, *Korean*) rather than linear co-occurrence restriction. This is because the consonant in C_1 is ill-formed in Korean such that Koreans tend to perceive a vowel inserted between $C_1.C_2$ as a repair strategy in perception of English consonant clusters. Although the experiment in the current chapter does not use English consonant clusters as stimuli, the tendency to count extra syllables in syllable final segments of the words seems to relate to perceptual vowel epenthesis.

Additional Syllable Counts by Way of Vowel Epenthesis

As mentioned, the current results show that Korean speakers' syllable counts of bisyllabic English words are sensitive to the inherent quality of word-final segments. That is, bisyllabic English words with final obstruents tend to be counted as having more than two syllables by way of vowel epenthesis after word-final obstruents. On the other hand, bisyllabic English words ending with sonorants are counted as bisyllabic. In relation to second language acquisition (i.e., the acquisition of English by Koreans), Lee (1998) points out the asymmetry between obstruent and sonorant final segments in terms of vowel epenthesis: "1) an epenthetic vowel is under duress in the presence of obstruents 2) on the other hand, the sonorant coda disallows an epenthetic vowel" (p.739) .The asymmetric patterns in interlanguage between the two categories (obstruents vs. sonorants) are shown in (4).

(4) Asymmetric vowel epenthesis between final obstruents and sonorants in interlanguage by Koreans (adapted from Lee, 1998, p. 739)

a. target	interlanguage	b. target	interlanguage
bit	bit^{h}ɨ	sin	sinØ *sinɨ
mid	midɨ	seal	sealØ *sealɨ
bus	busɨ	mom	momØ *momɨ

The reason why a vowel is inserted after a word final segment may come from a preference for the unmarked CV syllable structure in Korean: A vowel is inserted "to serve a function to convert a coda consonant into onset and to result in less marked syllable structure CV.CV" (Lee, 1998, p.739). However, this unmarked (or universal) CV syllable structure preference is not enough to account for why word-final sonorants (in CVC syllale structure) disallow vowel epenthesis while word-final obstruents tend to insert a vowel at the end of words in interlanguage, thus, ending in a CV.CV structure from CVC) as shown in (4). In addition, it is necessary to explain why not all word-final obstruents allow an epenthetic vowel at the end of words as shown in (5).

(5) Variations of vowel epenthesis in interlanguage (adapted from Lim, 2003)

English	Interlanguage by Koreans
a. book	buk˺ *bu.k^{h}ɨ
b. mook	mu.k^{h}ɨ, *muk˺
c. bed	be.dɨ, *bet˺
d. cut	cu.t^{h}ɨ, or cut˺
e. seat	si.t^{h}ɨ, or si.it˺, *sit˺
f. sit	sit˺, *si.t^{h}ɨ
g. pyramid	p^{h}i.ra.mi.dɨ or p^{h}i.ra.mit˺

(T^{h}: aspirated; T˺: unreleased)

Then, what determines vowel epenthesis after word final stops in interlanguage by Koreans? Is it the voicing of the coda stop? Is it the length of the vowel that precedes the stop? Or, is it the number of syllables in the word? There have been some efforts to account for variations in vowel epenthesis after word-final obstruents in loanword phonology. Yoo (1996) and Lee (1998) suggest that the voicing of the final stops is one of the major factors in vowel epenthesis. In addition, the importance of the place of articulation of the final stops is raised in Kang (1996) and Lee (1998). Furthermore, there is a correlation between vowel epenthesis and the tenseness of the vowel that precedes the final stops (Hirano, 1994; Yoo, 1996; Lee, 1998). The relevance of the number of syllables to vowel epenthesis was reported in Hirano (1994) and Kim (2000). Finally, in Kang (1996) and Kim (2000), it is shown that the placement of stops within words and the following vowel affect vowel epenthesis. The factors relevant to vowel epenthesis noted in previous studies are summarized in Rhee and Choi (2001) as shown in (6).

(6) Major factors related to vowel epenthesis in loanword phonology (adapted from Rhee & Choi, 2001)

a. the voicing of the coda stops:
voiced final stops (85%) > voiceless final stops (34%)

b. the place of articulation of coda stops:
coronals (64%) > velars (39%) > labials (23%)

c. the tenseness of the preceding vowels of coda stops:
tensed preceding vowels (88%) > lax preceding vowels (22%)

d. the number of syllables in the word:
monosyllables (64%) > bisyllables (34%) > trisyllables (33%) > four syllables and more (29%)

e. the placement of stops within words and the following context effect:
word-medial pre-sonorants (85%) > word final (50%) > word-medial pre-obstruents (19%)

Rhee and Choi (2001) argue for the arbitrariness of vowel epenthesis in loanword phonology, and thus, that epenthetic patterns cannot be accounted for by rules or constraints.[42] Rather, they look for the interdependency between the above-mentioned five major factors and vowel epenthesis from a statistical observation of 409 words found in newspapers and journals. As a result, they succeed in obtaining an equation with about 90% prediction of vowel epenthesis after coda stops as shown in (7).

(7) Rhee and Choi (2001)'s equation for vowel epenthesis in loanwords

E(logit) = -4.384 + (4.124 * voicing) + (1.955 * stop-placement 1) + (0.726 * stop-placement 2) + (5.214 * word-medial context 1) + (1.675 * word-medial context 2) + (3.202 * preceding vowel tenseness) + (-.368 * syllable numbers)

As shown in the equation, the voicing of the coda stops, word-medial pre-consonant context (i.e., word-medial context 1 above), and the tenseness of the preceding vowel are highly correlated with vowel epenthesis in loanwords from English. In addition, the number of syllables in the words is negatively correlated with epenthesis: The more syllables within words, the less often vowel epenthesis tends to occur.

Based on 5,000 loanwords from English compiled by the National Academy of the Korean Language, Kang (2003) proposes that vowel insertion is motivated to improve the perceptual similiarity between the English input and the Korean output as well as to obey a morphophonemic restriction in Korean:

Based on the result of the survey, it is proposed that the motivation of

42 Optimality theoretic analyses may capture why a vowel is epenthesized and why there is an asymmetry between coda stops and sonorants in terms of vowel epenthesis with the interaction of universal markedness constraints and faithfulness constraints (cf. Kang, 1996; Kang, 1996; Lee, 1998; Lee, 2001). However, it is still not easy to account for the arbitrary patterns of vowel epenthesis even under the OT framework.

vowel insertion is the maximisation of the perceptual similarity between the English input and the Korean output, as well as a morphophonemic restriction in Korean. Specifically, it is proposed that post-stop vowel insertion yields a good perceptual approximation to stop release and, given the fact that final stops are more frequently released after a tense vowel than after a lax vowel in English, that perceptual similarity considerations account for the vowel-tense effect; post-stop vowel insertion brings the Korean output closer to the voiced stops of English, due to phonetic processes in Korean such as intervocalic voicing of plain stops and open syllable lengthening of vowels. On the other hand, the higher frequency of vowel insertion after coronal stops is attributed to morphophonemic restrictions on underlying /t/-final nouns in Korean. (p. 220)

Representations of English Words in Korean Orthography[43]

As previously mentioned, syllable counts were tabulated from the Korean orthographic representation made by the Korean participants mainly because Korean orthography captures nicely the internal syllable divisions within words. However, first, we must consider the way in which English segments are perceived and thus represented in Korean orthography.

Representation of English /l/ and /r/ in Korean Orthography

We begin with the question of how Korean speakers perceive English /l/ and /r/, and then look at how they represent these two in their own orthographic representation. In American English, /l/ and /r/ are two separate phonemes, which are contrastive in every prosodic position as shown in (8).

(8) American English /l/ and /r/ in various phonological positions (from Han, 2002: 694)

a. word-initial position right vs. light

43 For representing English loanwords with Korean orthography, see Appendix B.

b. consonant cluster position	pray vs. play
c. intervocalic position	arrive vs. alive
d. word-final position	poor vs. pool

Unlike English, Korean has only one liquid transcribed as /L/ in its phoneme inventory with two allophones : 1) a flap [ɾ], and 2) a lateral [l]. Distribution of these allophones is predictable: [ɾ] for syllable-initial position and [l] for syllable-final position, respectively. That is, the [l] and [ɾ] in Korean are in complementary distribution; thus they never overlap with each other in terms of distribution. Regarding the perception of English /l/ and /r/ by native speakers of Korean, there are several questions to be answered. Do Korean speakers perceive English /l/ differently from English /r/? Do Korean speakers perceive syllable-final /l/ better than syllable-initial /l/ in English? The latter question is based on the distribution of the liquid in Korean phonology. If that is the case, do Korean speakers perceive English syllable-initial /r/ better than syllable-final /r/ as well? It has been reported that phonological and phonetic differences in liquids between Korean and English cause Korean speakers some difficulty in producing as well as perceiving the English /l/ and /r/ due to what they call 'L1 transfer or interference effect' (Borden et al., 1983; Sakow & McNutt, 1993; Ingram & Park, 1998).

Let us now consider how Koreans represent the English /l/ and /r/ with their own orthography. As mentioned, on the surface (or phonetic) level, Korean does not allow consonant clusters either syllable initially or finally such that we can maximally have CVC structure if we only think of monosyllabic words in Korean. Therefore, we consider the Korean orthographic representation of the English /l/ and /r/ in syllable initial and final positions only as shown below.

(9) Korean orthography for English /l/ and /r/ by syllable position

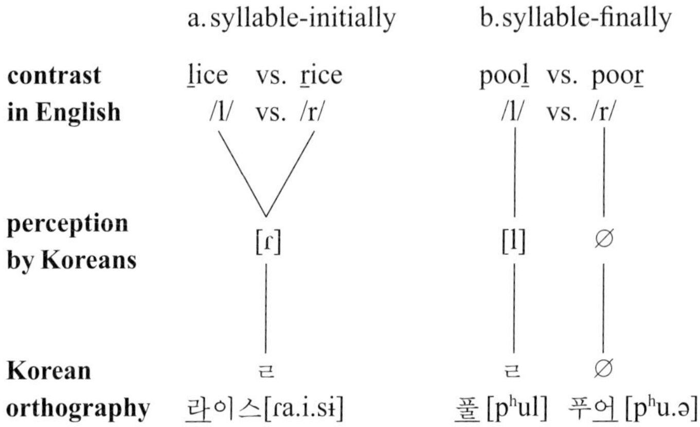

As shown in (9a), the contrastive English /l/ and /r/ in syllable initial position are represented using the same symbol 'ㄹ' regardless of their phonetic differences in English. As for the syllable-final position, however, only English /l/ is represented with Korean orthographic representation 'ㄹ', while English /r/ is deleted and/or replaced by a vowel [ə] as seen in (9b). Depending on syllable position, the contrastive /l/ and /r/ in English may be perceived differently by Koreans, and thus, their representation in Korean orthography is made, accordingly. In the following subsection, we will discuss how the voicing contrast in English stops are represented in Korean orthography.

Representation of English /p/ and /b/ in Korean Orthography[44]

In Korean, there is no voicing contrast and all stops are voiceless regardless of their syllable position. Unlike binary voicing contrasts in English, however, Korean has a three-way distinction in syllable-initial stops: 1) lax stops ㅂ, ㄷ, ㄱ transcribed as /p, t, k/, 2) tense stops ㅃ, ㄸ, ㄲ transcribed as /p', t', k'/ and 3) aspirated stops ㅍ, ㅌ, ㅋ transcribed as /p^h, t^h, k^h/. This three-way contrast disappears in syllable-final posi-

44 For Korean orthographic effects on perception of English voicing contrasts, see Chapter 6.

tion where the contrast is claimed to be neutralized[45](Martin, 1951; Lee, 1972; Kim-Renaud, 1974; C.W. Kim, 1979; Chung, 1980).

This raises the question of how Korean orthography represents the two-way, *voiced vs. voiceless*, English voicing contrasts, which are not contrastive in Korean phonology. Korean orthographic representations of English /p/ and /b/ in syllable-initial and syllable-final positions can be seen in (10).

(10) Korean orthography for English /p/ and /b/ by syllable position

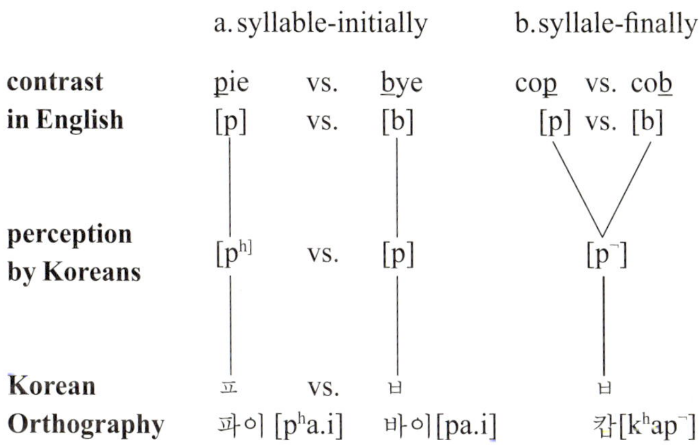

As shown in (10a), Korean orthography reflects the voicing contrast between English /p/ and /b/in the syllable-initial position with its different orthographic symbols: i.e., 'ㅍ' for /p/ and 'ㅂ' for /b/. However, syllable-finally, it seems that the voicing contrast, */p/ vs. /b/*, in English is not captured in Korean orthography, and thus, the syllable final English /p/ and /b/ are represented as the same with the symbol 'ㅂ', as shown in (10b). Korean orthography expresses the voicing contrast in English not in terms of voicing, but, rather, in terms of aspiration difference between /p/ and /b/. In addition, it seems that coda neutralization in Korean phonology affects Koreans' perception of English voicing contrast in syllable final position, and thus, the English contrast /p/ and /b/ in the

45 For coda (or syllable final) neutralization, see Chapter 6.

syllable-final position results in being represented with a neutralized form ' ㅂ ' in Korean orthography.[46]

Syllabification and Syllable Counts

Korean phonology can predict the syllabification of certain sounds based on their distribution. That is, the perceived [l]-like sound is highly likely to be affiliated with syllable-final position because the [l] in Korean is strictly distributed only in the syllable-finally position. On the other hand, [pʰ] and [p] tend to be in the syllable-initial position while the [p˺] tends to be syllable-final due to its distribution in Korean phonology. Thus, the syllabification of a sound can be predicted based on the distribution as shown in (11).

(11) Distribution and syllabification in Korean

	distribution	**predicted syllabification**
a. [l]	coda	Vl → Vl.
b. [pʰ]	onset	Vpʰ → V.pʰ
c. [p]	onset	Vp → V.p
d. [p˺]	coda	Vp˺ → Vp˺.

('V': vowel; '.' : syllable boundary; 'C˺': unleased stop)

To complete the syllable structure CV, a vowel may need to be inserted after a certain sound, which eventually contributes to additional syllable counts as shown in (12).

(12) Syllabification, vowel epenthesis and syllable counts

	distribution	**syllabification**	**vowel epenthesis**	**syllable count**
a. [l]	coda	Vl → Vl.	no	1
b. [pʰ]	onset	Vpʰ → V.pʰ	yes: V.pʰV̲	2
c. [p]	onset	Vp → V.p	yes: V.pV̲	2
d. [p˺]	coda	Vp˺ → Vp˺.	no	1

(V̲: inserted vowel)

The syllabification patterns observed in Korean shown in (11) and (12) may also apply when English words are parsed by Korean speakers. In English, an initial or a final stop in CVC syllable structure can maintain its contrastive features such as voicing (e.g. [pin] vs. [bin]; [bet] vs. [bed]). In Korean, however, contrasting features can be maintained in syllable-initial positions (e.g., 풀[pʰul] 'grass' vs. 불[pul] 'fire' vs. 뿔 [p'ul] 'horn') whereas the contrastive features of a final stop in CVC in Korean must be neutralized due to a syllable-final stop neutralization phenomenon in Korean (e.g., 잎 ipʰ 'leaf' and 입 ip 'mouth' are neutralized into [ip˺]). Thus, in order to keep the English voicing contrasts in Korean, the contrasts should be placed in the syllable-initial position. Therefore, an alternative way to preserve word-final voicing contrasts in "bet" and "bed" in Korean is through syllable restructuring by way of vowel epenthesis at the end of the words as schematized in (13).

(13) Two strategies: keeping contrasts vs. keeping syllable structure

***Strategy A**: keeping voicing contrasts through vowel epenthesis*

bed → [pe.dɨ] 베-드 (2 syllables)
bet → [pe.tʰɨ] 베-트 (2 syllables)
C_1VC_2 → $C_1V.C_2\underline{V}$

↖ Vowel epenthesis at the end of words

***Strategy B**: keeping syllable structure*

C_1VC_2 → C_1VC_2
pull → [pʰul] 풀 (1 syllable)
pin → [pʰin] 핀 (1 syllable)

Keeping the voicing contrasts in English (e.g., 't' vs. 'd'), word-final English stops are represented in Korean orthography (e.g.,'ㅌ' for 't' and 'ㄷ' for 'd') by way of an addition of vowel to the end of the words, and this violates the syllable structure (*Strategy A*: $C_1VC_2 \rightarrow C_1V.C_2\underline{V}$). This

46 This possible coda neutralization effect will be explored in detail in Chapter 6.

restructuring of word-final stops (as onsets of the following syllables) results in the addition of an extra syllable to the syllable count, whereas more sonorous final segments such as nasals and liquids maintain syllable structure, which leads to the syllables being counted as they are (*Strategy B:* $C_1VC_2 \rightarrow C_1VC_2$).

Syllable Counts and Perception of Syllables and Contrasts

The syllable counting explored in this chapter involves many steps and processes in terms of production, perception,and orthographic representations as shown in Figure 3.2.

Figure 3.2. Production of English words perceived by Koreans, and represented with Korean orthography

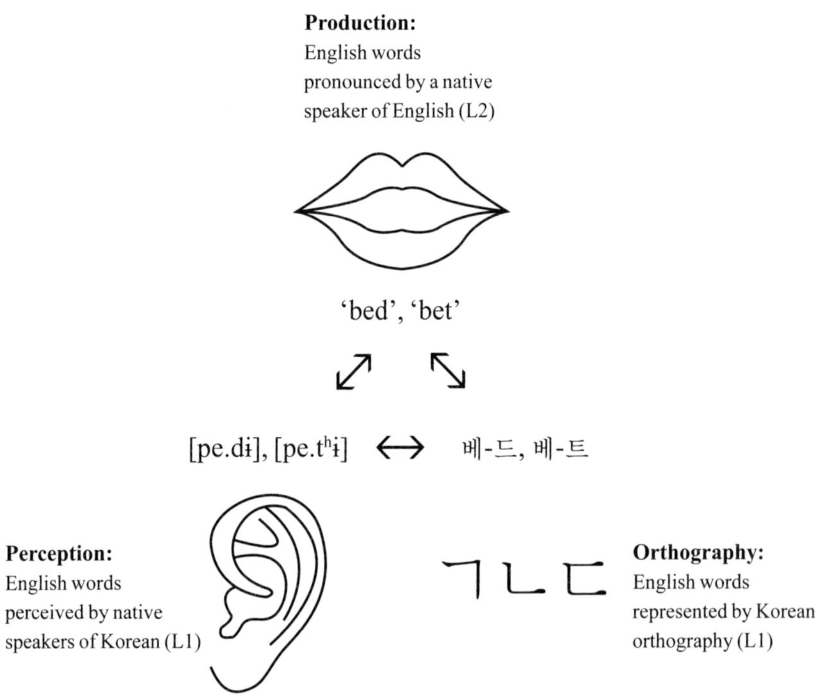

As shown, voicing contrast in English is maintained, and thus, accurately perceived to the ears of Korean speakers. And yet, the native speakers of Korean may have to pay a price for this perception process. That is, the syllable position where the contrast is situated, i.e., *syllable-final*, is switched into a new position, *syllable initial*, by way of vowel epenthesis. This 'perceptual switch' of syllable affiliation, i.e., *from final (VC) to initial (CV)*, may help Korean speakers better perceive the voicing contrast of the English words. Still, some immediate questions remain to be answered: Does this perceptual switch come from the strong CV-syllable based syllabification strategy manifested in Korean? Or, is this shift due to the universal syllable prime CV in language? To what degree, does L1 perception and/or orthography play a role in perception of L2 contrasts and syllable affiliations? Especially, from L2 learners' perspectives, what are the dynamics between and within these processes? As an effort to answer some of the questions raised in this chapter, I will look deeper into the relationships and dynamics of these processes in the following chapters.

Summary

In Chapter 3, a typological approach was introduced to examine the relationship between syllabification and syllable counts. Generally, English speakers seem to be able to say how many syllables are contained in a word without much difficulty whereas they have somewhat more difficulty saying where each syllable starts or ends (cf. Abercrombie, 1967; Erickson, Akahane-Yamada, Tajima, & Matsumoto, 1999). On the other hand, Korean speakers rarely indicate ambiguous syllable divisions of English words while they are inconsistent with counting the syllables of the English words. Given this, the current chapter aimed to further investigate syllable counts of English words by Koreans. In so doing, relevant factors for English syllabification including stress-placement, the phonetic nature of word-final segments, and word-final vowel quality were manipulated for the experiment. Findings showed that Koreans' syllable counts were sensitive to word-final segments: Bisyllabic English words with final stops tend to be counted as having more than two syllables while words ending with either a nasal or liquid are usually counted as bisyllabic. It was also shown that word-final diphthongs only, but not word-final tense vowels, tend to be counted as two separate vowels by Korean listeners. These syllable counts and syllabification of English words by Koreans are summarized in (14).

(14) Syllabification and syllable counts of English words by Koreans

CVCV	→	CV.CV	if the final vowel is either lax or tense
	↘	CV.CV.V	if the final vowel is diphthongal
CVCVC	→	CV.CVC	if the final consonant is a nasal or liquid
	↘	CV.CV.C(V)	if the final consonant is a stop

↖ vowel epenthesis → ***CV syllable-based***

(C: consonant; V: vowel; '.': syllable boundary)

Considering a hypothesis in which "rhythm is considered a central organizing factor in speech perception and production" (Erickson et al., 1999, p. 1479), the inconsistency in syllable counting of English words by Koreans reported in Chapter 3 indicates that Korean listeners may have difficulty perceiving the basic rhythm-bearing units of English. As suggested in Erickson et al. (1999), L1 rhythmic units (i.e., CV-based syllable for Korean) may interfere with L2 rhythmic units (strong-syllable based for English: cf. Cutler & Norris, 1988) in perceiving the L2. These interactions will be further pursued in the next chapters.

CHAPTER 4

ENGLISH SPEAKERS' PERCEPTION OF SYLLABLES AND VOICING CONTRASTS

Introduction

The study presented in the previous chapter showed that Korean speakers seem to have no difficulty indicating where each syllable starts or ends in English words while they were quite different from native speakers of English regarding the ways in which they count the number of syllables in English words. Of those relevant factors for syllable counting, it seems that Koreans tend to be more sensitive to the phonetic nature of word-final segments (e.g., stops, nasals, liquid, or vowels). In relation to syllable counting, as a way of enhancing the perception of voicing contrast of the word-final segments (for exmaple, be<u>d</u> vs. be<u>t</u>), some Korean speakers perceive the words as if the words have a vowel inserted at the end of the final segments resulting in a switch in syllable affiliation (e.g., [pe.dɨ] for 'bed' and[pe.tʰɨ] for 'bet'). This "perceptual" switch of syllable affiliation of the final segments, *i.e., from syllable final to syllable initial*, may be a necessary step or process for some Koreans to perceive voicing contrasts in English, which are not contrastive in Korean phonology. One important question, then, is whether this switch comes from the strong CV-syllable based syllabification in Korean, or whether this perceptual switch is due to the universal prime CV syllable in language. Chapters 4 and 5 will address these issues.

Special Status of the CV Syllable Structure

Studies of segmentation units in continuous speech (e.g., Cutler & Norris, 1979; Savin & Bever, 1970; Segui, Frauenfelder, & Mehler, 1981) have found that listeners can extract syllabic units from continuous speech. Furthermore, at the syllable level, naïve listeners of English perceive dynamic modulation of syllable structures as a function of speech rate (de Jong, Lim & Nagao, 2001): Singleton coda consonants (VC syllable structure) are perceived as onset consonants (CV syllable structure) as speech rate increases. Stetson (1951) interprets this resyllabification effect as due to a simplification of a more difficult prosodic organization to a simpler one. This general line of interpretation would be indirectly supported by the cross-linguistic typology literature which notes the speical status of CV syllable structure (Greenberg, 1978): The CV syllable is the universal syllable type found in all known world languages (Jakobson, 1966); the CV syllable is the predominant form in infant babbling (Locke, 1983); syllable-initial consonants (in C̲V) seemed to be more tightly coordinated with the following vowel than are syllable-final consonants (in VC̲) with the preceding vowel (Browman & Goldstein, 1988; Ladefoged, 1982).

Uncovering the nonlinear relationship between acoustics and perception and between articulatioin and acoustics, Tuller and Kelso (1990, 1991) demonstrate that naturally occuring linear changes in articulation (e.g., relative phase of glottal and oral movements) are perceived as categorical changes in the location of syllable juncture (i.e., perceptual shift from VC to CV syllable). Arguing for the relative stability of CV over VC, Tuller and Kelso (1990) indicate that vowel-consonant syllables shift to the consonant-vowel form, but not vice versa, suggesting that the CV syllable structure is intrinsically more stable.

Cross-language studies (Lim, de Jong & Nagao, 2001; Nagao, Lim & de Jong, 2001) on this rate-induced resyllabification have shown that non-native speakers of English, *Korean and Japanese speakers specifically*, perceive this dynamic resyllabification (from VC to CV syllable structure) in a pattern similar to that reported by English speakers (de Jong et al.,2001) suggesting that perceptual resyllabification is a uniform phenomenon that seems to be independent of individual language characteristics.

However, perception of syllabification has also been shown to occur in a very language-specific manner as well. In a series of studies on segmentation by infants (Jusczyk, 1997; Jusczyk, Friederici, Wessels, Svenkerud, & Jusczyk, 1993; Mattys, Jusczyk, Luce, & Morgan, 1999), parsing speech was shown to be dependent on the rhythmic structure of languages (e.g., strong-syllable-rhythm-based segmentation for English; mora-rhythm-based segmentation for Japanese; syllable-rhythm-based segmentation for French). The rhythm-based segmentation strategy can be detected during the first year of life. That is, 9-month-olds can hear a repetitive occurrence of rhythmic patterns in a language with which they can separate the speech strings into chunks. They also listen longer to speech with high transition probabilities between speech sounds than to speech with low transition probabilities (Jusczyk, Luce, & Charles-Luce, 1994). In other words, infants seem to be very sensitive to factors around the boundaries in the speech, including phonotactic constraints (Mattys & Jusczyk, 2001; Jusczyk et al., 1993; Jusczyk et al., 1994), allophonic variations (Hohne & Jusczyk, 1994; Jusczyk et al., 1999), probabilistic frequencies (Saffran, Aslin, & Newport, 1996), and prosodic regularities (Jusczyk et al., 1993; Mattys, Jusczyk, Luce, & Morgan, 1999).

Chapter 3 indicates that Korean listeners may have difficulty perceiving the basic rhythm-bearing units of English, possibly due to interference from L1 segmentation units (i.e., CV-syllable based units for Korean shown from Chapter 2) with L2 rhythmic units (strong-syllable-based units for English: cf. Cutler & Norris, 1988). In Chapters 4 and 5, I employ a new paradigm, *a repetitive speech task*, to examine the relationship between production and perception under systematically varied conditions. The perception of repetitive speech is investigated in order to probe the perceptual patterns of dynamic modulation of syllable structure as a function of speech (cf. de Jong 2001a, 2001b). Replicating and extending studies of Stetson (1951) and Tuller and Kelso (1990, 1991), de Jong (2001a) shows that, in production experiments where Midwest English speakers produced repetitions of CV and VC syllables in time to a metronome pacer which systematically changed in period (from slower to faster), durational patterns for CV and VC syllables are very different at slow rates whereas the patterns tend to converge at fast rates (to CV structure).

In the following chapters, in order to examine the "special status" of CV syllable structure which may be more important in syllabification in Korean or more "universal" in any language, I will re-examine an observation by Stetson (1951) that singleton coda consonants (VC syllable structure) are perceived as onset consonants (CV syllable structure) as speech rate increases by closely looking at English speakers (in Chapter 4) and Korean speakers (in Chapter 5). In so doing, I will use repetitive speech with systematically controlled rates as did in de Jong (2001a, 2001b). This research presented in Chapter 4 will serve as a baseline experiment for further arguments in Chapters 5 and 6.

Experiment

Methods

The current experiment examines perceptual shifts in prosodic organization (i.e., syllable affiliation) as a function of speech rate in English. It also investigates perceptual shifts in phonetic category classification of voicing contrasts in relation to syllable affiliation, i.e., onset or coda, to investigate the dependencies and interactions between perceptions of a stop's affiliation and its voicing contrast in repetitive speech production.

Participants

Twenty-three native speakers of English participated as listeners in the experiment. They were all students at Indiana University and were paid for their participation. All were monolingual speakers of Midwest American English with no previous history of speech or hearing problems. Since five participants provided inconsistent responses (see procedures below), their responses were excluded, and only 18 participants were analyzed.

Stimuli

The stimuli for the experiment were extracted from a production experiment in de Jong (2001a, 2001b): One female (AH) and one male (KD), both native speakers of midwestern varieties of American English repetitively produced syllables with voiced and voiceless labial stops (i.e., /b, p/) in pre-vocalic (onset) and post-vocalic (coda) position as shown in Table 4.1.

Table 4.1. Stimuli

	voiced stop	**voiceless** stop
onset structure	'bee' [bi]	'pea' [pi]
coda structure	'eeb' [ib]	'eep' [ip]

Repetitive speech production was systematically controlled by using a metronome with increasing rates starting from slow (450ms/syllable) to fast rate (200ms/syllable). Each stimulus included three repetitions of one of the four monosyllables, 'bee', 'pea', 'eeb', and 'eep', and thus, there were a total of 168 stimuli (21 rate-varied stimuli (from slow to fast rates) * 2 speakers * 4 monosyllables: for details concerning the production of repetitive speech, see de Jong 2001a, 2001b). Figure 4.1 presents a schematic representation of rate-varied stimuli for the experiment.

Figure 4.1. A schematic representation of rate-varied stimuli

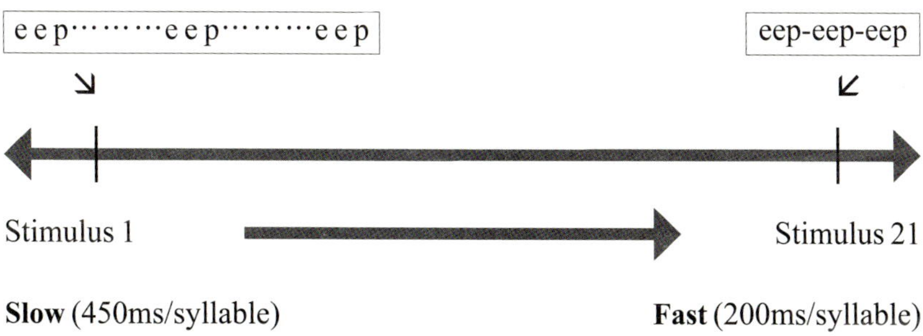

Procedure

The listeners were asked to identify what they heard after the stimuli were presented to them through headphones. There were four choices, labeled as 'bee', 'pea', 'eeb', and 'eep', from which the listeners would make their best choice for each stimulus by clicking a mouse on a computer screen.

Prior to the experiment, there was a brief practice session in which eight trials were given to familiarize the listeners with the task. Throughout the trial sessions, none of the participants reported any difficulty with the task. To check internal consistency in their responses, the listeners were presented with additional stimuli at the end of the session. On the basis of this post-test check, five inconsistent listeners were excluded, leaving a sample of 18 participants for analysis.

Results

Figure 4.2 shows the percentage of identifications as CV's (represented with diamonds) or as voiceless (represented with squares) from the input 'eeb' as a function of rate. That is, the figure shows how the listeners identified stimuli as CV's ('pea', or 'bee') and as /p/ ('pea' or 'eep') from the intended productions of 'eeb.' The horizontal scale indicates the location of the stimulus in the original utterance, ranging from slow repetitions on the left to fast on the right.

For the identification of syllable affiliation, 100% means the listeners identify the stimuli 100% as "CV syllable structure" while 0% indicates they identify them 0% as "CV syllable structure" (or, 100% as VC). As for the voicing identification, 100% means the listeners identify the voicing of the stimuli 100% as /p/ while 0% indicates they identify them 0% as /p/ (or, 100% as /b/).

Figure 4. 2. Identification of syllable affiliation and voicing from input 'eeb'

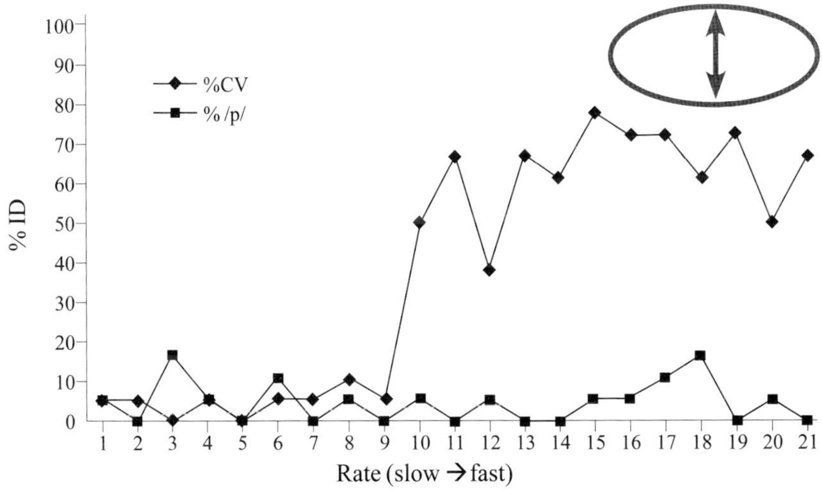

As for the identification of syllable affiliation, the diamond symbols indicate the correctly identified VC syllable structures as intended from the input 'eeb' at slower rates (shown as lower percentage, or closer to 0%, as CV to the left in the figure); then there is a shift toward CV responses as the rate increases (to the right in the figure). For voicing identification, the stimuli 'eeb' were consistently identified as /b/ as shown closer to 0% across the range of rates.

The highlighted data in the circle in Figure 4.2 raises the question of why the fastest rate tokens are not identified as resyllabified (as CV from the stimuli 'eeb') 100% of the time, but rather at a level of 75% at best. de Jong, Lim and Nagao's (2004) acoustic models suggest that this incomplete resyllabification at fast rates is due to differences between the speakers' utterances as well as interlistener differences in the degree to which they hear the fast VC stimuli as being resyllabified.

Another intriguing issue concerns the interaction between the two identification patterns: The identification of syllable affiliation and voicing. Figure 4.3 shows these identification patterns from the input 'eep' as a function of rate.

Figure 4.3. Identification of syllable affiliation and voicing from input 'eep'

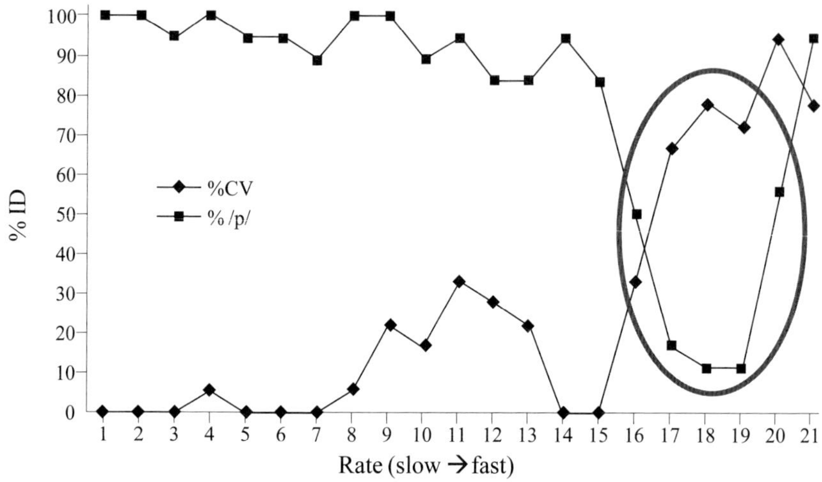

Figure 4.3 shows that there is also a resyllabification effect at fast rates from the input 'eep' even though there was a difference in points at which resyllabification (i.e., VC to CV) began to occur compared to the input 'eeb' in Figure 4.2. However, one noticeable difference between inputs 'eeb' and 'eep' lies in the patterns of voicing perception. That is, as shown in Figure 4.3, identification of voicing /p/in the input 'eep' was almost 100% /p/ at slower rates, while it tends to be perceived as /b/ at faster rates as shown as lower /p/ percentage (to the right of the figure). In contrast, voicing identification of the input 'eeb' was well identified as /b/ regardless of rate change.

Note that the temporal points, at which resyllabification (i.e., from VC to CV) occurred, correspond to the points where voicing shifts as marked with a circle in the figure (points numbered 17 through 21). At faster rates, the listeners misidentified the intended input 'eep' regarding both its syllable affiliation and voicing. That is, the listeners might think they heard 'bee' (or 'bee-like') from the production of fast-rate repetitions of 'eep.'

So far I have shown perceptual patterns of resyllabification from VC productions (i.e., stimuli 'eeb' and 'eep') with an interaction of voicing contrasts. As reported in de Jong et al.(2004), temporal dynamics seem to make perception of syllable affiliations in both CV and VC productions ambiguous at fast rates even though the listeners also seem to detect acoustic differences between fast rate CV and VC productions. Thus, I turn to the interaction between syllable affiliation perception and voicing identification from CV productions (i.e., stimuli 'bee' and 'pea').

Figure 4.4. Identification of syllable affiliation and voicing from input 'bee'

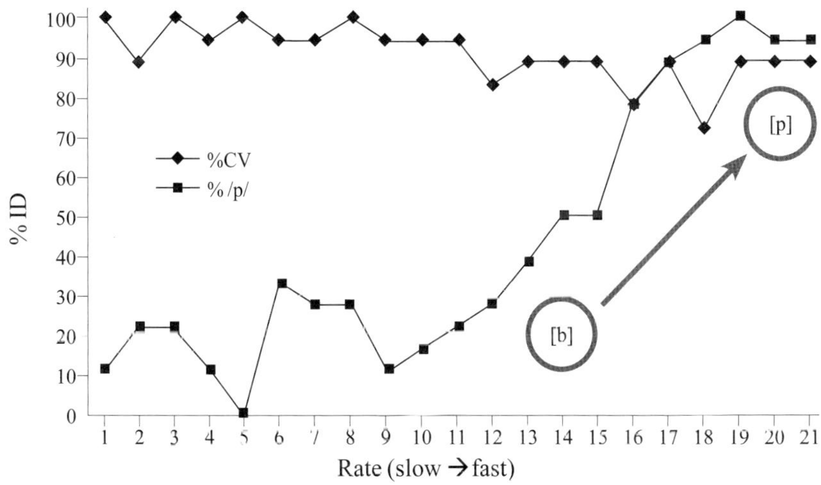

Figure 4.4 shows how participants identified the syllabification and voicing of the input 'bee'. It can be seen that identification of syllable affiliation was almost 100% CV at both slow and fast rates, although it is not as consistently identified as CV at fast rates. Interestingly, identification of voicing undergoes a drastic shift as rate increases. That is, the input 'bee' is perceived as /b/ at slow rates but tends to be perceived as /p/ at fast rates.

Finally, Figure 4.5 shows identification patterns of syllable affiliation and voicing of the input 'pea'.

Figure 4.5. Identification of syllable affiliation and voicing from input 'pea'

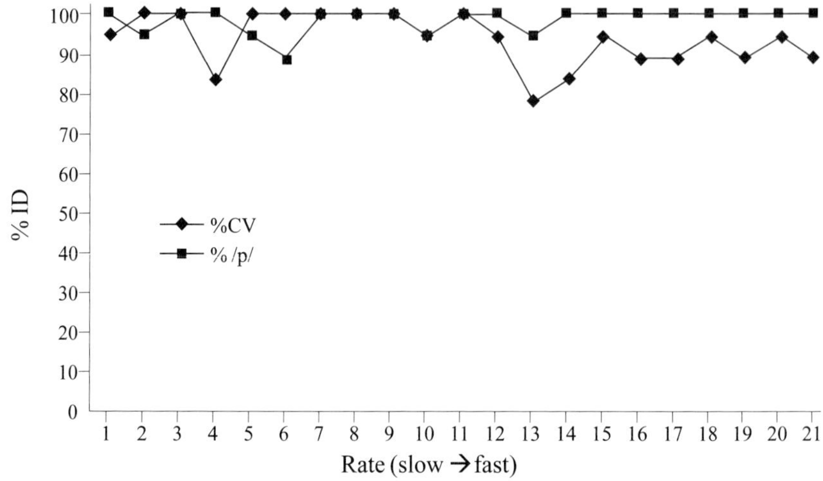

Similar to the case of 'bee', syllable affiliation was consistently identified as CV at slower rates while its percentage as CV slightly decreased at faster rates. Unlike the pattern of voicing identification of 'bee', however, the identification of voicing remained 100%/p/ regardless of rate change.

Discussion

So far I have shown the identification patterns of 18 American speakers of syllable affiliation and voicing and their interactions from both CV ('bee' and 'pea') and VC productions ('eeb' and 'eep'), and how these identification patterns are affected by the rate of speech (i.e., slow to fast), which is summarized in Table 4.2 below.

There are several points to be noted. First, results confirm findings from previous studies (Stetson, 1951; Tuller & Kelso, 1991; de Jong, 2001a & 2001b) that there is a prosodic reorganization (or *simplification*) to CV from VC syllable structures as speech rate increases. This resyllabification phenomenon could be driven by universally prevalent

CV (onset) syllable structures compared to relatively less frequent VC (coda) syllable structures cross-linguistically (cf. Greenberg, 1978). That is, this could be an influence from universal tendencies toward an unmarked syllable structure, CV syllable structure, in syllable parsing.

Table 4.2. A summary table for 18 American speakers' perceptual patterns of syllable affiliation and voicing contrast as a function of rate

input (or stimuli)	identifeid at slow rates	identified at fast rates	change from slow to fast rates
'eeb'	as VC	**as CV**	· prosodic reorganization from VC to CV
	as /b/	as /b/	
'eep'	as VC	**as CV**	· prosodic reorganization from VC to CV · voicing shift from /p/ to /b/
	as /p/	**as /b/**	
'bee'	as CV	as CV	· voicing shift from /b/ to /p/
	as /b/	**as /p/**	
'pea'	as CV	as CV	· no change
	as /p/	as /p/	

Another possibility is that, as suggested in Tarone (1984), there may be two different levels regarding syllable parsing; that is, syllable boundaries which operate at the phonological level may be different from the syllable boundaries which operate in the process of articulating an utterance. Along this line, Kozhevnikov and Chistovich (1965) suggested that there is some evidence that syllable divisions which are operative at the articulatory/perceptual level may be different from the syllable divisions which operate at the linguistic level: "When speakers were under stress in production or perception, they tended to break down the consonant clusters into CV patterns" (p.71). If I took this stance and assumed that a repetitive speech-production task causes the listeners to rely only on the articulatory/perceptual level, not on the linguistic/phonological level in the processing of syllables, then, as reported in the current study, the resyllabification effect could be a result of syllable parsing on the articulatory or perceptual level in which unmarked and universal CV structures predominate.

Second, a comparison of syllable affiliation identifications of the inputs 'eeb' (in Figure 4.2) and 'eep' (in Figure 4.3) raises another interesting question concerning the degree to which resyllabification occurred at faster rates when it comes to an interaction with voicing identification: Are VC structures with voiceless coda stops (i.e., 'eep') more likely to be resyllabified as CV structures than voiced counterparts (i.e., 'eeb')? A possible answer can be found in a regression model in de Jong et al. (2004) since the model suggests the degree of resyllabification is associated with phonemic voicing contrasts, the presence of voicing in the stop closure and the duration of the vowel. In particular, the regression model shows that in the VC productions of 'eeb,' longer vowels before /b/ (compared to the vowel duration before /p/ in 'eep') encourage VC identification at fast rates.

Third, voicing identification seems to be dependent on prosodic structures, but not the other way around (i.e., consonant voicing does not affect syllabification perception). Examining listeners' perception of voicing reveals a tendency to identify onsets as voiceless and codas as voiced. In particular, a closer examination of voicing identification of 'eep' is noteworthy in that the temporal locations at which resyllabification occurred correspond to the points where voicing identification of /p/ shifted to /b/ as shown in Figure 4.3. That is, perceptual shifts in voicing are matched to the perception of resyllabification of 'eep'. Therefore, in regards to voicing identification as presented in this study, there are several questions to be answered: Why do the listeners tend to identify the onsets (from stimuli 'bee' and 'pea') as voiceless and the codas (from stimuli 'eeb' and 'eep') as voiced as speech rate increases? If the perceptual shift in voicing of 'eep' occurs as a result of resyllabification at fast rates, why should it be /b/-like, why not /p/-like? Furthermore, it is striking that voicing identification of 'bee', which is a prosodically stable CV structure, shift to /p/ as speech rate increases. As suggested in de Jong et al. (2004), the temporal dynamics of fast rate speech influence even the stable CV (input) structures, since many of the fast rate tokens become ambiguous. In fact, as reported in de Jong (2001a), it seems that listeners detect some acoustic differences between the fast rate CV and VC productions, since most of them are more likely to identify the CV inputs as CV's than they are the VC inputs.

As for perception of voicing in stops, periodicity in the speech signal is a critical voicing cue. However, there are several important voicing cues other than periodicity: Voice onset time (VOT), the presence and the amplitude of aspiration noise and durational cues. Many of the primary cues to voicing seem to vary with the syllabic position of the consonant. In English, for example, voiced stops often have no vocal fold vibration, especially, in the syllable final position, which suggests that listeners should rely on other voicing cues such as temporal (and spectral) properties of the preceding vowel in post-vocalic stops (Soli, 1982). For syllable initial stops, the primary cue seems to be VOT; in general, a short or negative (or *voice lead*) VOT is a cue to voicing while a long VOT is a cue to voicelessness (Lisker & Abramson, 1964, 1970). Stop closure duration is a primary voicing cue for intervocalic stop consonants: A longer closure duration is a cuc to voiceless while a shorter closure duration is a cue to voicing (Lisker, 1957). When primary acoustic cues to voicing are ambiguous, spectra and F0 can affect voicing perception in CV sequences (Massaro & Oden, 1980). Furthermore, even for a stop consonant in a given syllabic position, numerous cues seem to contribute to the identification of the intended voicing (e.g., F1 transition after the onset of voicing (Lisker, 1957), and the fundamental frequency contour after voicing onset (Haggard, Ambler, & Callow, 1970)). Given that the stimuli used in the current study varied in speech rate, identification of voicing would be a more complicated task. Thus, the task requires that the listeners must be more sensitive to various cues in the speech signal and be able to integrate these cues to make a final judgment of voicing. In order to look more closely at perceptual shifts in voicing and to answer the questions addressed above, the acoustic measures were plotted from the production data in de Jong (2001a, 2001b) as a function of rate as follows.

Figure 4.6. Acoustic measures of CV structures ('bee' and 'pea') as a function of rate

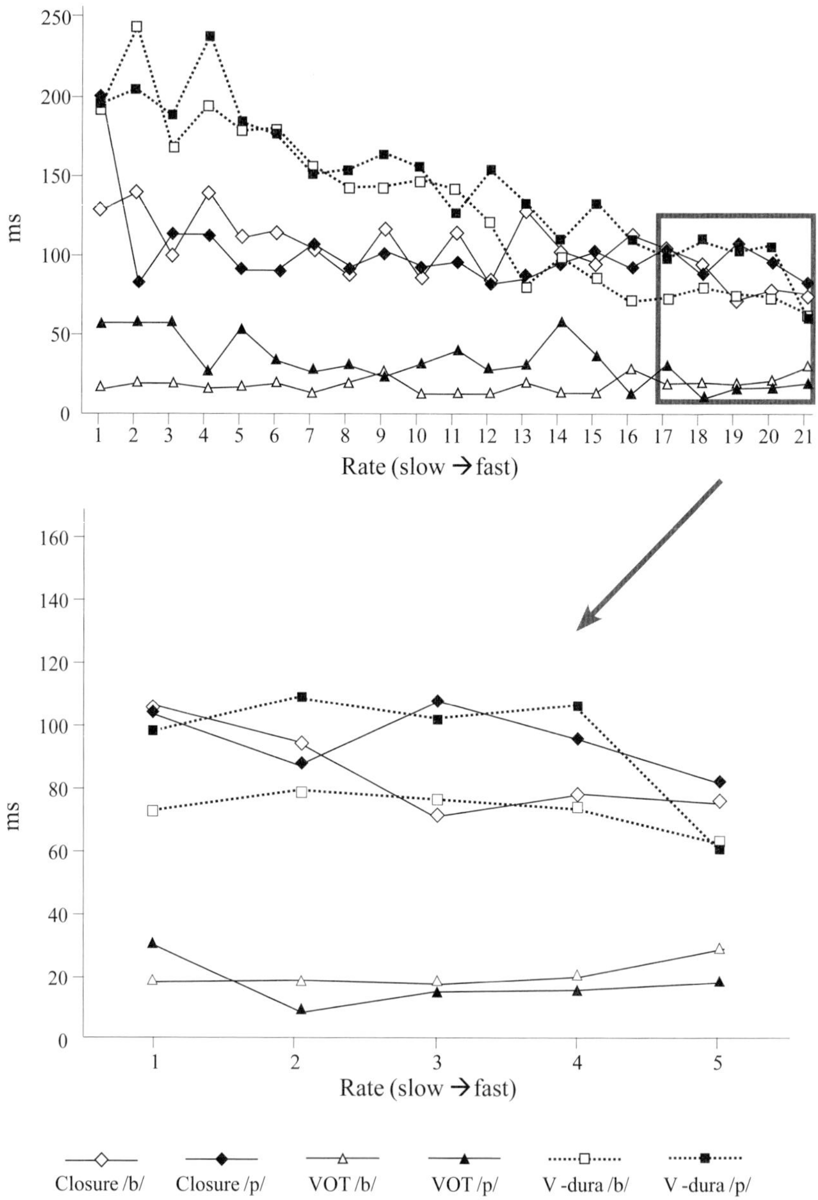

Figure 4.7. Acoustic measures of VC structures ('eeb' and 'eep') as a function of rate

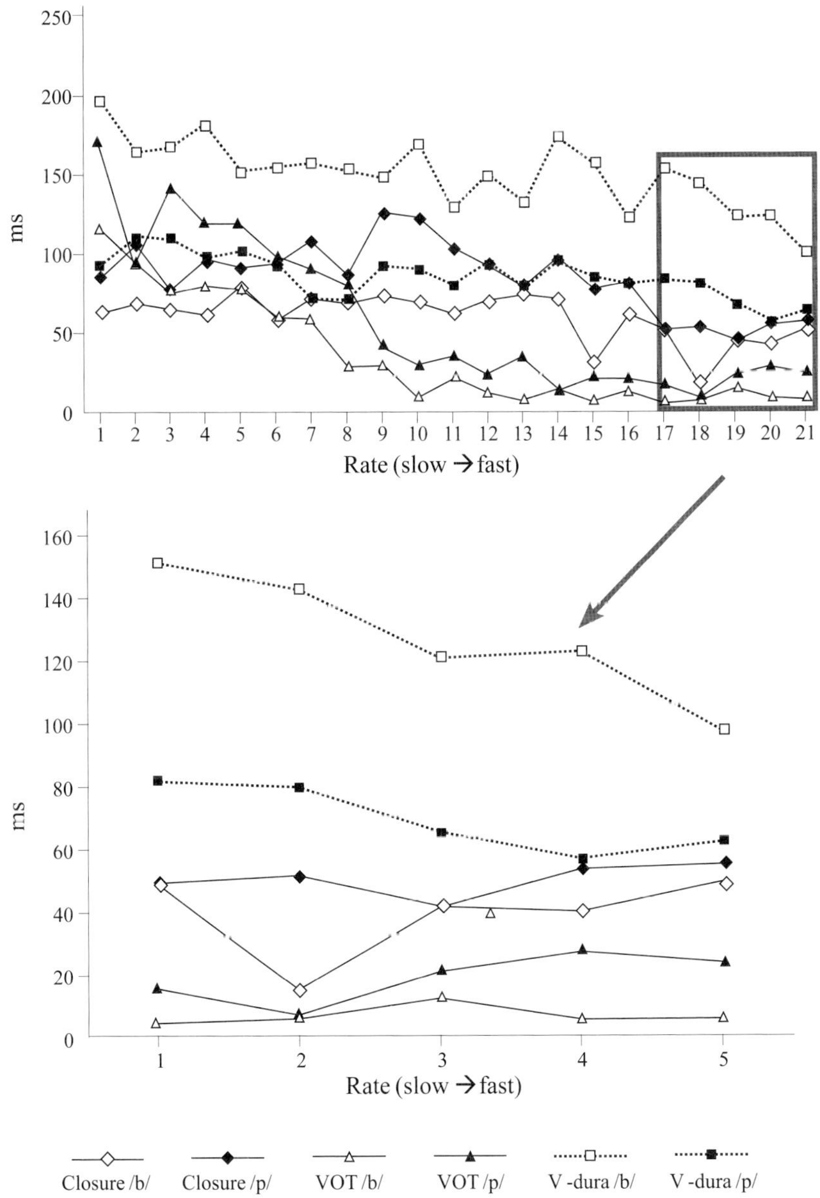

Figures 4.6 and 4.7 show acoustic measures of CV ('bee' and 'pea') and VC ('eeb' and 'eep') productions as a function of rate, respectively, which include stop closure duration, VOT, and vowel duration. In each figure, the top panel plots these acoustic measures against the whole range of stimuli (slow to fast) while the bottom panel plots them against only the faster stimuli numbered 17 through 21 (faster to fastest) to examine more closely the temporal dynamics at faster rates.

First, I turn to the question of why listeners misidentify the voicing of /b/ in 'bee' as /p/ as speech rate increases. As shown in the bottom panel of Figure 4.6, VOT values for the intended inputs 'bee' and 'pea' become identical at the fastest stimuli along with almost identical but slightly different closure durations between /b/ and /p/. In English, speakers use the stop closure interval differently depending on the position of the stop within the syllable. For example, in the syllable initial position, English speakers do not show a difference in closure duration between voiceless and voiced stops so they produce each stop with the similar closure duration (Crystal & House, 1988). Given the similar values of VOT and closure durations between the inputs 'bee' and 'pea' at faster rates, it is still not clear why the listeners perceived the voicing of /b/ in 'bee' as /p/ as speech was speeded up. However, if we consider that changes in speech rate can produce large effects on the duration of stop closure intervals, we may find a clue for this perceptual shift in the voicing of 'bee'. As is known, lengthening of the silent closure interval of a medial stop can produce the perception of voicelessness (Lisker, 1957; Port, 1976). Port (1979) further showed that closure duration of a medial stop as a voicing cue must be defined relative to speaking tempo; specifically, "the voicing cue is determined primarily by the ratio of the stop closure duration to the preceding vowel duration" (p. 53). The stimuli used in the experiment consist of three repetitions of four monosyllables ('bee', 'pea', 'eeb', 'eep'), and the listeners seemed to consistently focus on the middle portions of the repeated syllables (de Jong et al.,2004). Nevertheless, if the parsing windows are overlapped for voicing identification (or even identification of syllable affiliation) from repeated speech at faster rates, the listeners' task can be an identification of voicing in VCV environments, not necessarily in CV or VC only. If this is the case, the relative ratio of the stop closure duration to vowel duration can be a cue to voicing for the inputs 'bee'. Thus, the relative ratio of the stop closure duration to the preceding vowel duration against speech rates were plotted as in Figure 4.8.

Figure 4.8. Ratio of closure/vowel for 'bee' and 'pea' as a function of rate

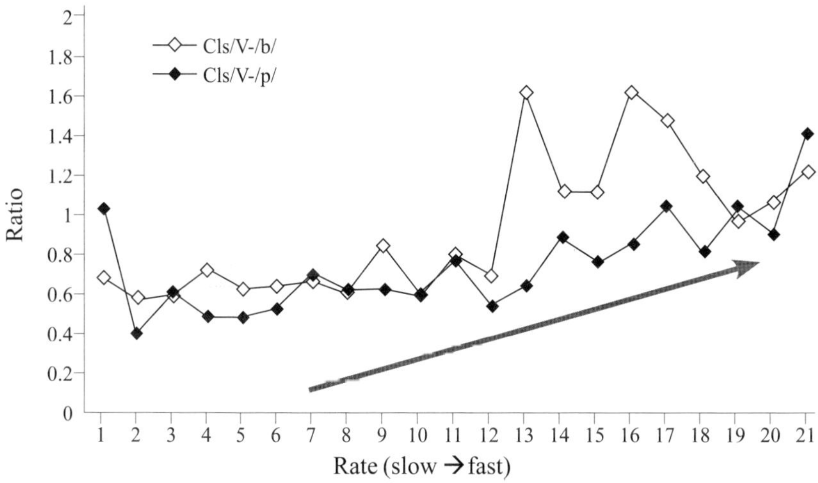

Compared to slower rates, faster rates show an increasing ratio of stop closure to vowel for both 'bee' and 'pea', which may cause the listeners to perceive lengthening of the closure interval. This increased ratio appears to provide the explanation for why listeners misperceive the voicing of 'bee' as /p/.

Now, then, turn to the acoustic measures of VC productions ('eeb' and 'eep') as shown in Figure 4.7. Naturally, all values of acoustic measurements decrease as speech rate increases. Especially, longer VOT values of both 'eeb' and 'eep' at slow rates, which include syllable junctures, drastically diminish at faster rates. If we recall that the inputs 'eep' have shown the resyllabification effect occurring after the stimulus #16 as in Figure 4.3, the listeners began to misidentify the intended coda /p/ as onset /b/ starting with stimulus #17. The bottom panel in Figure

4.7 shows that the VOT value of the intended 'eeb' remains near zero while the VOT value of 'eep' is less than or near 20 milliseconds at the fastest rates. On the other hand, the values of stop closure duration of the intended inputs 'eeb' and 'eep' become almost identical at faster rates. Regarding effects of speech tempo on the VOT boundary, Summerfield (1974, 1975) has shown that listeners use information about speech tempo when judging a particular VOT value signaling a voiced or voiceless stop. That is, the VOT boundary between voiced and voiceless consonants shifts toward lower values as speech is speeded up. Given that VOT is a primary cue to voicing for syllable initial consonants, and the resyllabification effect holds in the VC productions ('eeb' and 'eep) at faster rates, the smaller values of VOT could be a possible contributor to identifying voicing of 'eep' (as well as 'eeb') as /b/. Furthermore, as Miller (1981) suggested, for a certain phonetic distinction, such as voicing, the listeners must process the tempo-dependent cues such as consonant closure duration and vowel duration in relation to the rate of speech at which they are produced. Then, the concept of C/V ratio as a cue for the voicing features (Port & Dalby, 1982) may play a role in making a final judgment in voicing at faster rates in our repetitive

Figure 4.9. Ratio of closure/vowel for 'eeb' and 'eep' as a function of rate

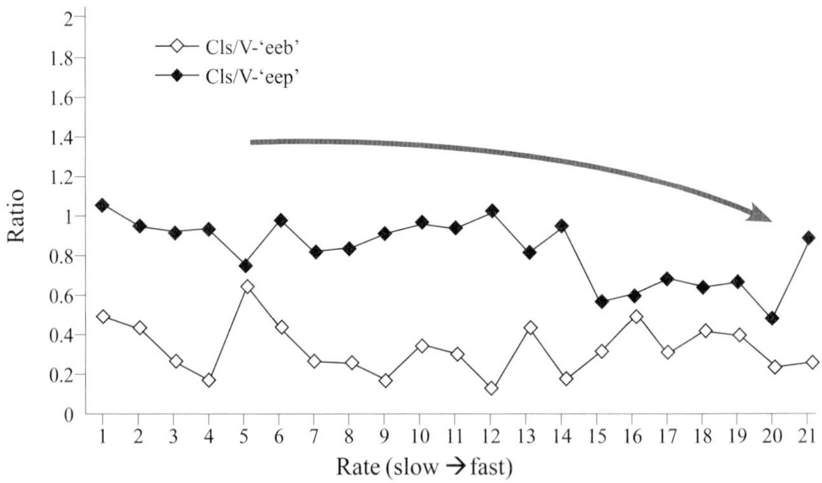

productions. Along this line of reasoning, Figure 4.9 shows the relative ratio of the stop closure duration to the preceding vowel duration (C/V ratio) for the intended inputs 'eeb' and 'eep' as a function of rate.

In particular, 'eep' has more rate effects in stop closure duration than in the preceding vowel duration as speech rate increases. Thus, the listeners may pick up on the greater reduction in stop closure duration relative to the preceding vowel duration as a shortening of the closure interval, which could mislead them to make a final judgment of the /p/ in 'eep' as /b/ at faster rates.

Summary

Prior to investigating perceptual patterns of syllable affiliation and voicing contrasts by Korean learners of English (Chapters 5 and 6), Chapter 4, as a baseline study, probes perception of repetitive speech by native speakers of American English to examine perceptual patterns of dynamic modulation of syllable structure as a function of speech (cf. de Jong, 2001a, 2001b). In so doing, repetitive speech production was systematically controlled by using a metronome with increasing rates starting from slow rates (450ms/syllable) and increasing to fast rates (200ms/syllable). Each stimulus including three repetitions of one of the four monosyllables, 'bee', 'pea', 'eeb', 'eep', was played to 18 American students attending Indiana University in order to identify a baseline understanding of how syllable affiliation and voicing are incluenced by speech rate.

The results confirmed Stetson's (1951) observation that singleton coda consonants (VC syllable structures) are perceived as onset consonants (CV syllable structures) as speech rate increases. Interestingly, identification of voicing showed a drastic shift as rate increases. That is, the initial consonant in 'bee' was perceived as /b/ at slow rates, but at fast rates was perceived as /p/. In addition, the final consonant of 'eep' was perceived as /p/ at slow rates but shifted to /b/ as rates increased. On the other hand, voicing identifications of the inputs 'pea' and 'eeb' were well identified as /p/ and /b/ respectively regardless of rate change. Taken together, it seems that the perception of voicing contrasts is dependent on the perception of syllable affiliation but not the other way around (i.e., consonant voicing does not affect syllabification perception).

Having shown, thus far, perceptual patterns of syllable affiliation and voicing contrasts by American listeners, I now move on to the second language perception of syllabification and voicing contrasts by closely examining the perceptions of repetitive speech by Korean learners of English in the following chapters (Chapters 5 and 6).

CHAPTER 5

SECOND LANGUAGE PERCEPTION OF SYLLABLES AND VOICING CONTRASTS

Introduction

In Chapter 4, I have shown perceptual patterns of syllable affiliation and voicing contrasts by 18 native speakers of Midwest American English through an experiment using repetive speech tasks where repeated speech production (i.e., eep-eep-eep; eeb-eeb-eeb; pea-pea-pea; bee-bee-bee) was systematically controlled by a metronome with increasing rates from slow (450ms/syllable) to fast (200ms/syllable) rates. Results show that, as speech rate increases, coda consonants in VC syllable structures (e.g., 'eep' and 'eeb') are perceived as onset consonants (CV syllable structures). This finding is similar to the idea of '*rate-induced resyllabification (or simplification)*, as reported in previous studies (Stetson, 1951; Kelso & Tuller, 1990, 1991; de Jong 2001a, 2001b). As for the interaction between syllable affiliation and voicing contrasts, it seems that the perception of voicing contrasts is dependent on the perception of syllable affiliation but not the other way around.

Given these findings as a baseline, the current chapter investigates perceptual patterns of syllable affiliation and voicing contrasts by non-native speakers of English whose native language differs from English with regard to the types of syllable structures and their phonetic voicing category. It also probes the effects of the degree of exposure to the target language on perception of syllables and voicing contrasts in repetitive speech by examining two different L2 learner groups: 1) more exposed learners of English who spent at least one semester studying in the United States and 2) less exposed learners of English whose English learning had been limited to language learning in their home-country.

Effects of Language Background on Perception

In the field of second language acquisition, attention has been given to the role of the syllable in interlanguage pronunciation. Tarone (1984) addressed the issues concerning the relationship of the syllable structures of the native language (L1) and the target language (L2), and raised a question of how L1 and L2 should be incorporated into contrastive analyses. She also echoed the question raised in Tarone (1972) (cf. Hooper, 1977) regarding whether there is a universal or 'unmarked' syllable structure, and how such a phenomenon might affect second language acquisition (p. 64). Since the current chapter is concerned with second language learners' perception of the rate-induced resyllabification in L2 speech, there are some questions to be answered as to whether the learner simply transfers his/her own L1 syllable structure into his/her perception of the L2 or if alternatively, regardless of L1 or L2 syllable structures, the rate-induced resyllabification phenomenon is driven by universal tendencies toward an unmarked syllable structure (i.e., the universality of the CV syllable structure in world languages (Tarone, 1976))?

Furthermore, since the current study also investigates Korean learners' perceptual patterns of voicing contrasts in repetitive speech produced in English, the phonetic voicing category of each language is also important. In English the series of stop phonemes are distinguished by the phonological feature *voicing*. On the other hand, stop consonants in Korean are not differentiated by the voicing feature since they are all classified as voiceless. That is, the phonemic differentiations between /b, d, g/ and /p, t, k/ are described as voiced vs. voiceless for the English language only. However, the voicing contrasts are clearly categorical, not phonetic. In English, for example, voiceless /p, t, k/ are articulated with voice onset times (VOT) which typically exceed 30-35 msec while voiced /b, d, g/ are produced with VOT values less than 35 msec. In Spanish, however, the voiceless stops /p, t, k/ are articulated with VOT values less than 35 msec, such that stop consonants with the same VOT values can be classified either as voiced (for English) or voiceless (for Spanish) depending on their phonetic voicing category in that language. Figure 5.1 illustrates phonetic category classification of English and Korean stop consonants in the syllable initial position. As shown, phonologically classified English voiced stops /b, d, g/ have phonetic VOT values which fall into the phonological classification as voiceless in Korean. Therefore, language specific phonctic voicing categories should play a role in the perception of voicing contrasts along with its interaction with temporal changes in speech production. These issues will be carefully considered in the current study, which analyzes the perception of the rate-varied repetitive speech tasks.

Figure 5.1. Phonetic category classification of English and Korean stop consonants in relation to average values of VOT (adapted from Zampini & Green 2001)

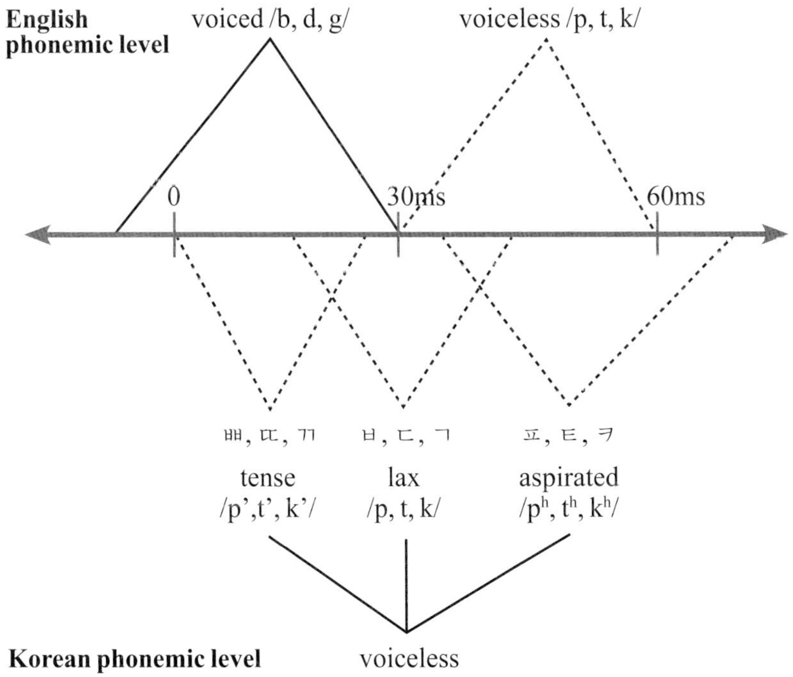

Effects of Exposure to L2 on Second Language Learning

First and second language research findings have shown considerable evidence that the age at which learners are initially exposed to a language is a robust predictor of their long-term success in the target language, particularly as to whether or not they can reach native-like abilities in the second language (Long, 1990). Another important factor relevant to this biological age factor is the amount of L2 input, since it is positively correlated with L2 performance. The more L2 input learners have, the more native-like their L2 performances will be. Therefore, the age of arrival (AOA) to the target environments is considered an important index measuring the amount of native L2 input. Since AOA is confounded with some uncontrolled variables, length of residence (LOR) in the L2 environment, in general, is used to index the amount of the L2 input (Flege, Yeni-Komshian,& Liu, 1999; Grenier, 1984; Oyama, 1982). However, some studies have failed to show that L2 performance improves as LOR increases (Flege et al., 1999; Piske, MacKay &Flege, 2001). Rather, LOR provides a good index of L2 input for some individuals but not others; for example, an LOR effect is greater for students than for non-students (Flege & Liu, 2001).

Hypotheses

The current experiment investigates Korean learners' perception of syllable affiliation and voicing contrasts in rate-varied repetitive English speech with both 'between' and 'within' language factors. First, *between languages*, a comparison was made with the perceptual patterns of native speakers of English, which is reported in the experiment in Chapter 4, in order to examine effects of language background on L2 perception. Second, *within languages*, Korean learners were categorized into two different groups according to their degree of exposure to English as indexed by LOR in order to see L2 exposure effects on perception in repetitive speech tasks. Based on these, I first hypothesize that listeners' perception of syllable affiliation relies on the complexity of syllable structures in their native languages when measured as the degree of resyllabification as a function of rate. Korean has relatively simpler syllable structures than English, and this relative simplicity in syllable structures means that simple CV forms predominate in Korean. This predominance might facilitate the Korean listeners' choosing CV syllable affiliation at faster rates, and thus, be reflected as more resyllabified responses to CV from original VC inputs compared to native speakers of English.

Alternatively, even though Korean syllable structures are different from English, Korean has both CV and VC syllable structures as does English, and thus, Korean listeners' perception of syllable affiliation might not be different from native speakers of English in terms of the degree of resyllabification. Both hypotheses are, more or less, based on the perception of a "universal" signal- driven resyllabification phenomenon, which is controlled by rate change in speech.

In regards to the perception of voicing contrasts, I hypothesize that voicing perception would be influenced by the listeners' phonetic voicing category in their own language. As shown in Figure 5.1, for syllable onset position, Korean has a three-way contrast in voiceless stops, and the boundary between aspirated and unaspirated stops has a longer VOT than the boundary between voiced and voiceless in English. Thus, we expect a bias in Korean listeners against perceiving items as aspirated in syllable onset position. On the other hand, predictions with respect to the voicing of coda consonants are much more complicated in Korean. Since Korean has the coda voicing neutralization[47] phenomenon toward voiceless, we might expect a bias toward voiceless responses from Korean listeners.

Finally, with respect to the effects of exposure to English, I hy-

---

47 Korean has a three-way contrast in syllable initial stops: lax stops /p, t, k/(ㅂ, ㄷ, ㄱ), tense stops /p', t', k'/(ㅃ, ㄸ, ㄲ) , and aspirated stops /p^h, t^h, k^h/(ㅍ, ㅌ, ㅋ) and this three-way contrast is neutralized into lax sops in the syllable final (or coda) position (Martin, 1951; Lee, 1972, Kim-Renaud, 1974; C.W. Kim, 1979; Chung, 1980). For detailed descriptions of syllable-final neutralization, or coda-neutralization, in Korean, see Chapter 6.

pothesize that the more exposure a participant has to the L2, the more native-like their perceptual patterns will be. Thus, we expect that Korean learners who have more exposure to English, compared to the Korean learners with less exposure, will show more similar perceptual patterns to native speakers of English in terms of perception of syllable affiliation and voicing contrasts.

Experiment

Participants

To control for an LOR effect on perceptual tasks in the experiment, as participants we used two student groups of Korean learners of English with different LORs in the United States: 1) those with significant exposure to English, i.e., who had spent at least one semester studying English (or using English for formal education) in the United States and 2) those with limited exposure whose English learning had been limited to language learning in the home-country, Korea. Table 5.1 summarizes the statistics of the participants who participated in the experiment.

Table 5.1. Participant statistics for Experiment

	higher exposure learners	**lower exposure learners**
participant number	13	20
LOR (Min – Max)	3.4 years (1-6)	0
age (Min – Max)	28 years (24-32)	23 (20-25)

(LOR: Length of Residence in the U.S.)

The group of high exposure Korean learners of English was recruited from the Korean student population at Indiana University while the other group of 20 less exposed Korean learners was recruited at Sejong University in Seoul, Korea. The higher exposure learner group had an average of 3.4 years of LOR with a range from one to six years while the group of less exposed learners whose English education was limited to their home country, Korea, and who had never resided in the US or any other English speaking country.[48] The perceptual responses of 18 English participants reported in Experiment 1 (in Chapter 4) are used in this present study as controls.

Stimuli and Procedure

The stimuli and procedures were the same as the experiment in Chapter 4. However, since I used Korean learners of English as listeners, written instructions with Korean orthography were also given to each participant before experimentation. Partly due to time and space constraints, the experiments with the less exposed learners of English were run individually using a personal laptop computer at Sejong University in Seoul, Korea, while the more exposed learners were tested in groups of seven or eight at a same time using a computer lab at Indiana University. Other than that, every procedure was identical across the two groups of Korean learners of English, as well as to the procedure used to elicit responses from the native English speakers reported in Chapter 4.

Results

Perception of English Syllable Affiliation by Koreans

To examine how Korean learners of English with varying degrees of exposure to English perceive the rate-induced English syllables, I compared the two groups of Korean learners of English with the different

48 Being a cosmopolitan city, Seoul has become a multi-lingual as well as multi-cultural international city where many people from various countries interact with Seoulites or with other foreigners, and their languages of communication vary, and yet, it is easily expected to be pre-dominantly English. Along this line, even the less exposed Korean learners of English in this chapter may have different degrees of exposure to English within Korea, but the current experiment could not control for these individual differences.

Figure 5.2. Perceptual identification of VC syllable inputs 'eeb' (top) and 'eep' (bottom) as CV's plotted against location of stimulus in an increasing speech rate trial (from slow to fast rates)

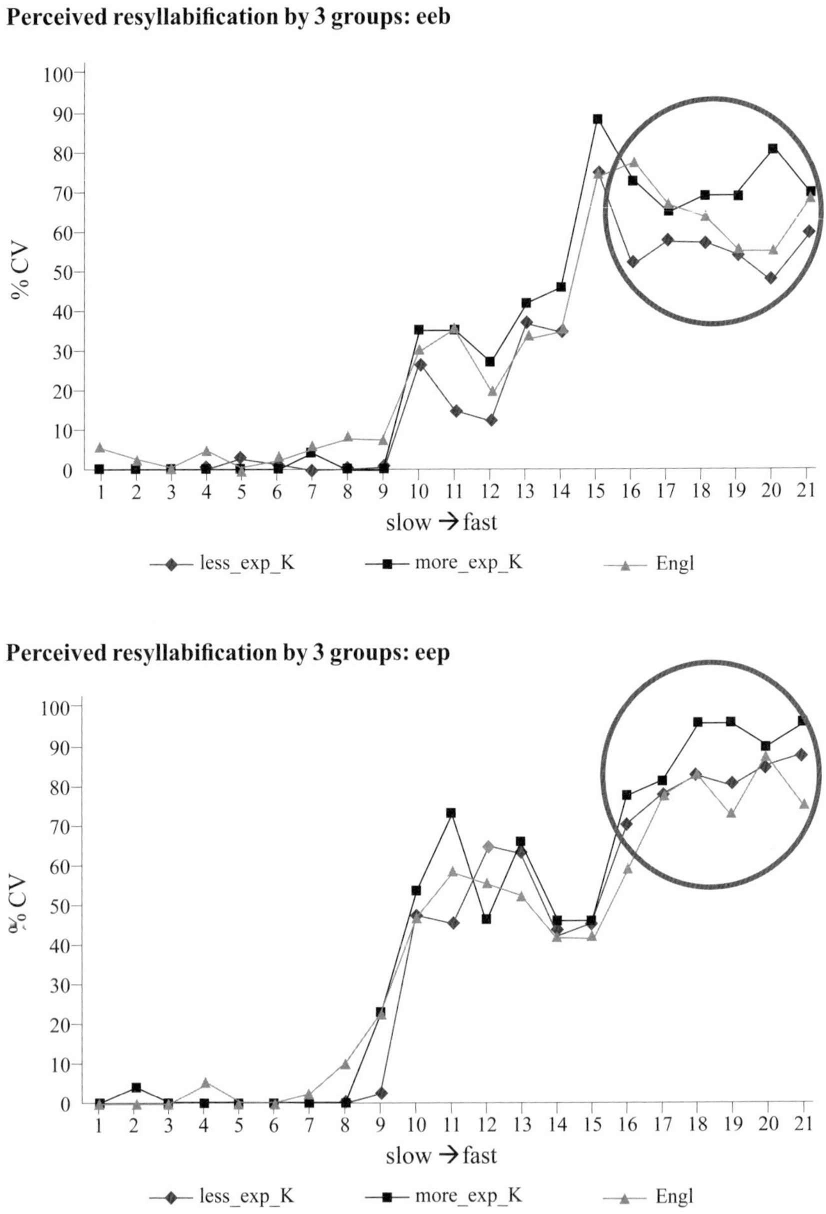

LORs. The first aspect of 'syllable perception' examined was syllable affiliation for VC structures (i.e., inputs 'eeb' or 'eep'). These results, for both Korean learner groups as well as the English control group, are reported in Figure 5.2. The top panel summarizes the patterns of resyllabification perception as a function of rate change by the three different groups for 'eeb' stimuli while the bottom panel shows perceptual responses to the stimuli 'eep'.

In the perception of VC tokens, all three groups - two groups of Korean learners and the English control group - exhibit resyllabification (i.e., perceive VC tokens as CV), and the category shift seems to occur at nearly the same location. Thus, the responses from all three groups are similar in shape and location. At faster rates,as highlighted in the circles (i.e., from rate points 16 through 21), a one-way ANOVA with percent perceived as CV syllable structure as the dependent variable and participant groups as the independent variable indicates that participant groups (i.e., 1) the less exposed Koreans vs. 2) the more exposed Koreans vs. 3) English controls) have a significant effect on the degree of resyllabification for the input 'eeb' [F (2, 15) = 6.816, $p = .008$], but not for the input 'eep' [F (2, 15) = 2.999, $p = .08$]. Post-hoc analysis for the input 'eeb' shows that only the more exposed Korean learners are significantly different from the less exposed Korean learners in terms of the degree of the resyllabification ($p = .006$).

Perception of English Voicing Contrasts by Koreans

I turn to the perception of the voicing contrast. I consider voicing perception for stops produced as onset stops (i.e., inputs 'pea', 'bee') separately from stops produced as codas (i.e., inputs 'eep', 'eeb').

Figure 5.3 shows voicing identification of stimuli for onset (CV syllable) structures (e.g., 'pea' or 'bee') by three groups: 1) less exposed Korean learners, 2) more exposed Korean learners, and 3) the native English speaking control group. Empty symbols indicate identification functions for the stimuli of voiceless onset 'pea' while filled symbols show for the identification of voicing in the corresponding voiced onset stimuli 'bee'.

First, for the 'pea' stimuli, English listeners are very good at identifying [p] in the syllable onset position with almost 95 % accuracy across all rates. The less exposed Korean learners, however, are not as good as the native English listeners at identifying [p], and they tended to perceive some voiceless tokens as voiced even at slower rates, as indicated in the upper left circle in Figure 5.3. More exposed Korean learners, however, are better at identifying [p] than the less exposed learners, which is more similar to the native listeners of English [$F(2, 15) = 53.522, p < .001$]. However, at faster rates neither group of Korean learners of English perform as well as the native listeners of English. In Figure 5.3 this can be seen in the upper right circle (i.e., 16 through 21 on the rate continuum) [$F(2, 15) = 5.892, p = .013$].

For the identification of voiced consonants in 'bee' stimuli, all three groups tended to hear /b/ as [p] as the speech rate increased. However, differences between groups reveal that a shift toward [p] occurred earlier for the English listeners than in either Korean learner group. While both Korean learner groups differed from the English listeners, the Korean groups were similar in their identification of voiced consonants (i.e., input 'bee') across all rates of speech; however, at the slower rates indicated in the lower left circle, there again is no difference between the groups in voicing identification [$F(2, 15) = .203, p = .819$]. Even at faster rates, there is no group difference in identification of voicing [$F(2, 15) = 3.217, p = .069$].

Figure 5.4 plots the identification of voicing for stop consonants in the coda position (i.e., 'eeb' and 'eep'). As shown, English listeners were generally very good at identifying voiced stops. This is indicated by the filled triangle symbols that reveal that less than 10% of the identifications are labeled as [p] across the rate continuum, which means more than 90 percent of the time English listeners perceived stops as voiced (i.e., as [b]). On the other hand, Korean learners seem to be less consistent in their tendency to hear voiced stops as voiceless both at slower rates and faster rates.

Figure 5.3. Identification of stops as [p] from CV stimuli ('pea' and 'bee'): Hollow symbols indicate percentage of voiceless stops; filled symbols indicated voiced stops.

Perception of Voicing: CV

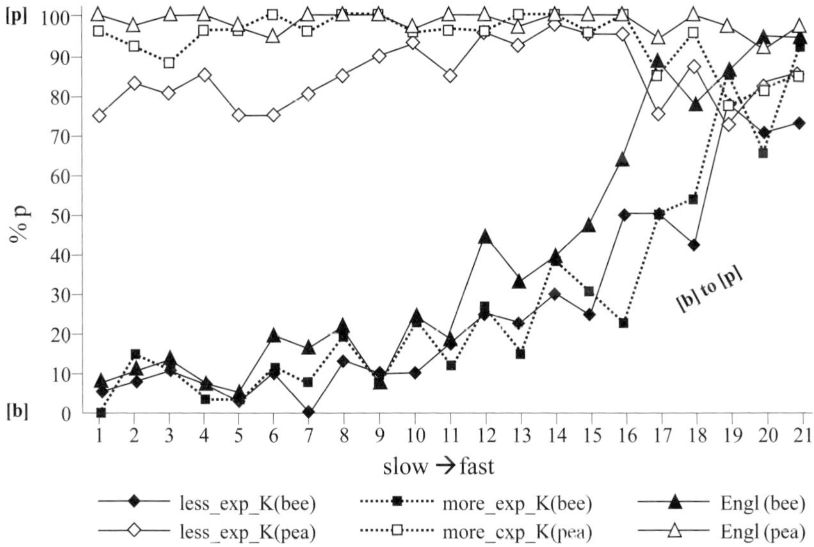

Figure 5.4. Identification of voicing contrast for VC stimuli: Symbols and axes are the same as in Figure 5.3.

Perception of Voicing: VC

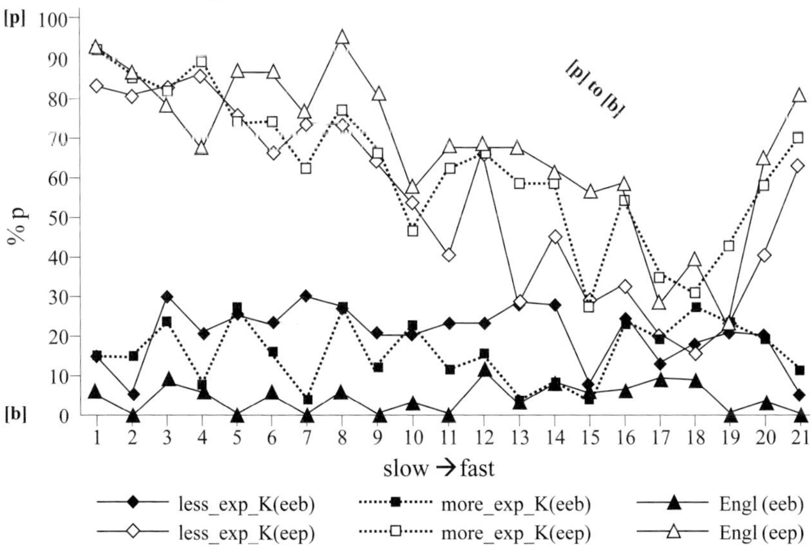

A one-way ANOVA shows that there is a significant group difference in voicing identification for the input 'eeb' both for the slower rates [F (2, 15) = 10.416, p = .001] and the faster rates [F (2, 15) = 11.336, p = .001]. Post-hoc analyses show that the English control group is different from both groups of Korean learners in their identification of [b] from 'eeb'.

For the identification of voiceless stops in 'eep' stimuli, all groups show that they tended to hear /p/ as [b] as speech rate increases. Interestingly, for the slower rates indicated in a circle, the less exposed Korean learners show a greater tendency toward [b] than the more exposed Korean learners, while the more exposed Korean learners are not significantly different from the English controls in their perception of /p/ in 'eep' [F (2, 15) = 5.707, p = .014].

Discussion

Language Background Effects on L2 Perception

Results show that there is also a resyllabification effect at fast rates from the VC stimuli ('eep' and 'eeb' inputs) in Korean learners' perceptual identifications of syllable affiliation. Interestingly, both more and less exposed learner groups shift to CV at nearly the same location in the rate continuum as native English-speaking listeners. This means that perceptual patterns of resyllabification in English as a function of rate are very similar whether or not listeners are native speakers of English.

However, it is still not clear whether this similarity is due more to categorical changes in the articulation of the stimuli, or due entirely to similarities in the perceptual boundaries for the listeners. Given this similarity, the fact that the Korean-speaking learners of English show relatively more complete resyllabification to CV structures from the VC stimuli at fast rates probably reflects the effects of native language syllable structures on the perception of target language syllables. Korean has simpler syllable structures than English, and the CV syllable structure accounts for a substantial portion of words in the language. In addition, as suggested in Chapters 2 and 3, the CV syllable structure, *as a rhythmic unit in Korean*, may play a significant role in the perception of rate-varied repetitive speech tasks in English. This could therefore bias the Korean listeners, *both more and less exposed*, to identify the fast-rated VC stimuli (i.e., 'eep' and 'eeb') more toward a CV syllable structure, compared to the English-speaking counterparts.

As for the effects of phonemic contrasts in native languages on voicing perception, although there is no voicing distinction in Korean phonology, Korean has a three-way distinction in syllable onset voiceless stops, which could be roughly analogous to the English voicing contrast. As such, Korean-speaking learners of English may have no difficulty picking up on the phonetic differences in English /p/ and /b/ such that they are generally good at identifying English voicing contrasts in the current stimuli. Furthermore, the phonetic categories in each language are different. For example, there are typically different category boundaries on a VOT continuum for each language as shown in Figure 5.1. This difference in voicing categorization seems to be reflected in subtle biases in the Koreans' responses. Koreans tend to require more aspiration for voiceless stops; for example, they tend to hear English /p/ more toward [b], especially in the syllable onset position as shown in the identification of voicing in 'pea' in Figure 5.3.

Of further importance is the fact that Korean listeners' identification of voicing contrasts is subject to the syllabic position of the stops: While native listeners of English were very good at identifying voiced coda stops, Korean listeners tend to show identification functions biased toward [p] even at slow rates (as shown at the bottom of Figure 5.4). This is probably due to the coda neutralization phenomenon in Korean where three distinct stops in onset positions are neutralized to unreleased lax stops in coda position. This possibility will be explored in more detail in Chapter 6.

Effects of L2 Exposure on Perception

With respect to effects of exposure to English on perception, I test the hypothesis that the more exposed to the L2 the learners are, the more native-like their perception of the L2. In so doing, I used two different groups of Korean learners, separated by their length of residence (LOR) in the United States *who are all late learners of English*. That is, the more exposed Korean learner group averaged 3.4 years of LOR while the less exposed Korean learner group has no LOR in any English speaking country at the time of participation in the current study.

Results of perception of syllable affiliation and voicing contrasts by two different Korean learner groups show that effects of L2 exposure on perception are observable such that the more exposed learners are more similar to native listeners of English. However, the effects are likely to be confounded with other factors, which are induced by speech rate change. For instance, the less exposed Korean learners were distinguished from the more exposed counterparts in their perceptual responses at slow rates while this perceptual distinction between the groups disappear, and thus, both Korean learner groups were similar at faster rates, which is different from native English listeners.

Another finding is that both learner groups were quite similar across all the rates such that they are distinguished from the native listener group (i.e., English controls) as observed in the perception of voicing from 'eeb' stimuli. In general, the more exposed learners were similar to native listeners or at least they are distinguished from the less exposed learners at slow rates whereas their perceptual identifications become more similar to the less exposed counterparts at faster rates. This suggests that the effects of L2 exposure may be maintained in the perception of L2 when L2 learners are under the situations in which the learners can use or rely on their newly established/acquired phonetic categories. As a result, they perceive L2 sounds correctly. However, when the learners are forced to be in confusing situations, such as identifying L2 sounds in fast repetitive speech, L1 biases become more evident.

Flege's Speech Learning Model and a Model for Bilinguals

Exploring extensively on the relationships between the production and perception of phonetic segments in a second language, Flege and his colleagues help provide insight into why adolescent or adult L2 learners differ from monoligual native speakers of the target L2 by proposing the Speech Learning Model (SLM). The SLM begins with two assumptions: "The first is that L2 Speech Learning is not constrained by a critical period. The second is that the capacities needed by monolingual children to learn the language specific properties of their L1 are preserved across the life span, and remain accessible to L2 learners of all ages" (Flege, 2007, p. 366). Based on his SLM, Flege (1995, 1998, 1999, 2002, 2003) suggests that as L1 phonetic categories develop through childhood and into adolescence, they become more likely to perceptually assimilate L2 speech sounds on a long-term basis, thereby resisting the formation of new categories for L2 sounds. Thus, the late L2 learners are expected to have some difficulty in producing authentic L2 sounds as well as perceiving them correctly until the new phonetic categories are established. Substantial amounts of L2 input may also be required for the acquisition of new categories for L2 sounds.

The SLM proposes that L1 and L2 phonetic subsystems of bilinguals "necessarily" interact, and the phonetic categories interact through mechanism called "*phonetic category assimilation*" and "*phonetic category dissimilation*." More specifically, a new phonetic category of an L2 sound will be blocked when neighboring L1 category areas are fully developed and when an L2 sound is perceived to be phonetically similar to an L1 sound. Then, L2 learners will at first use the closest L1 sound to produce L2 sounds, by "developing a composite category that merges the properties of the L1 and L2 categories that have been perceptually equated. Whereas, when a new category is established for an L2 speech sound in a portion of phonetic space occupied by an L1 sound, the new L2 category and the pre-existing L1 category may dissimilate from one another" (Flege, 2003, p. 330).

While most L2 research has focused on the effect of the L1 on L2 learning, *L1 interferece into L2*, the SLM suggests that phonetic interference between L1 and L2 is "bi-directional". Examining the production of English by 240 native Koreans with wide ranges of the age of arival (AOA), i.e., *who had arrived in the US between the ages of 1-23 years*, Flege, Yeni-Komshian, and Liu (1999) show that there is a strong correlation between AOA and foreign accent rated by English-speaking listeners: Native Koreans who had arrived in the US prior to the age of 12 years received significantly better ratings (i.e., better pronunciation of English) than those arriving after the age of 14 years. They show that all 240 native Koreans received significantly lower ratings than the native English monolinguals. Interestingly, even the groups who had lived in the US for an average of 20 years and had received all of their education in US schools had detectable foreign accents.

Yeni-Komshian, Flege, and Liu (2000), then, examined Korean sentences spoken by these 240 native Koreans and showed that a stronger L2 (English) effect on L1 (Korean) production in Korean-English bilinguals: Lower ratings (i.e., a bad pronunciation of Korean) were obtained for Korean sentences spoken by the group of early AOA bilingual Koreans. All of the groups, *early or late bilinguals*, received significantly lower ratings than the native Korean monolinugals, and, the early bilinguals who had arrived in the US before the age of 12 years old were perceived as producing the Korean sentence with an "American" foreign accent.

Since Lenneberg's (1967) introduction of a critical period of language acquisition, it seems that most tend to agree "the earlier the better", especially, for the acquisition of native-likeness production of an L2, although, the end point of the critical period is still controversial (e.g., 12-15 years for Scovel, 1988; Patkowski, 1989; 16-17 years for DeKeyser, 2000).

Given these findings and implications, I propose a model for bilinguals as shown in Figure 5.5.

Figure 5.5. A Model for bilinguals

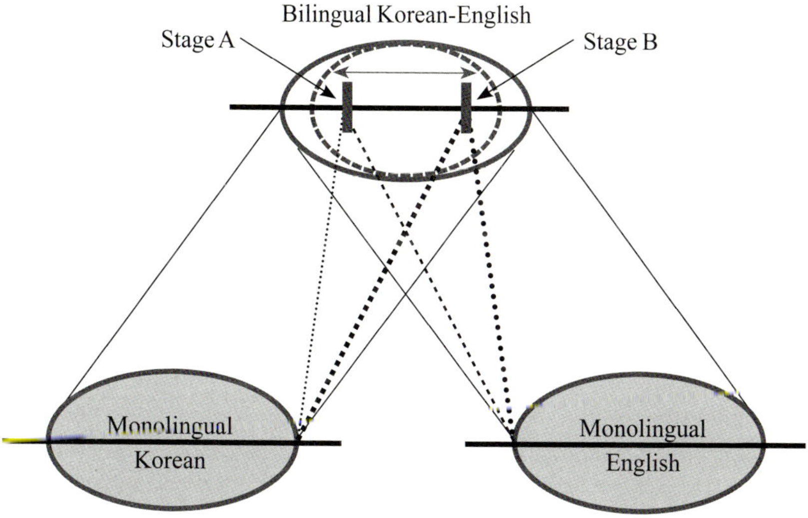

This model proposes that bilinguals share the phonetic categories of L1 and L2, and the different stages of acquisition of the L2 indicates a different degrees of language dominance by one of the languages. For example, Stage A indicates a bilingual whose English use and proficiency is stronger than Korean (e.g., Koreans who had arrived in the US prior to the age of 3 years and remained for at least 20 years) while Stage B shows a bilingual whose Korean is more dominant than English (e.g., Koreans who had arrived in the US at the age of 17 years and lived in the US for less than 6 years). As the L2 language acquisition process is dynamic and ongoing, it may continue for a life-time, which is represented by a dotted circle at the top of the figure. The dotted circle also indicates that successful bilinguals sound like native speakers of an L2, but they may still have "detectable foreign accents" to the ears of monolinguals.

Summary

Chapter 5 investigated perceptual patterns of syllable affiliation and voicing contrasts by Korean learners of English by employing a new paradigm, perception of repetitive speech (for details, see Chapter 4). In addition, it examined the effects of the degree of exposure to the target L2 language (English) on perception in repetitive speech by looking at two different Korean learner groups: 1) more exposed learners of English who lived and studied English in the US and 2) less exposed learners whose English learning had been limited to their home country, Korea.

Results showed that Korean-speaking learners of English perceived the dynamic resyllabification (from VC to CV) in a similar manner to English speakers. Furthermore, it was shown that the perception of resyllabification was done in a language-specific manner as well, influenced by the characteristics of language background. In particular, Korean-speaking learners of English show relatively more complete resyllabification to CV structures from the VC stimuli at fast rates. As suggested in Chapters 2 and 3, the CV syllable structure consists of a segmentation and rhythmic unit in Korean, which may bias Korean listeners to identify the fast-rated VC stimuli more toward CV structure.

Exposure to English seems to affect the perception of syllable structure and English voicing contrasts in repetitive speech in that the more exposed Korean learners of English perceive patterns of voicing identification in a manner more similar to native speakers of English than the less-exposed counterparts. However, the exposure effects can be confounded with other factors driven by speech rate change. More specifically, the less exposed learners were differentiated from the more exposed learners in their perceptual responses at slow rates by showing a bias toward [b] while this perceptual distinction disappears at faster rates, and thus, both learner groups were similar at faster rates. While the learner groups' performances converged at these faster rates, their performances diverged significantly from the English monolingual control group.

Findings in Chapter 5 show that Korean listeners' identification of voicing contrasts seems to be subject to the syllable position of the stops: Native speakers of English were very good at identifying voiced coda stops, while Korean-speaking listeners tended to show identification functions biased toward [p] even at slow rates. This may have to do with coda neutralization in Korean phonology where three distinct stops in the onset position are neutralized to unreleased lax stops in the coda position. This possibility will be further explored in connection with orthographic representations in Chapter 6.

CHAPTER 6

PHONOLOGY, ORTHOGRAPHY AND PERCEPTION OF NON-NATIVE CONTRASTS

Introduction

The previous chapter showed that Korean learners' perception of voicing contrasts in English stops (i.e., /p/ vs. /b/) seemed to be subject to syllable position of the stops. That is, in the identification experiment of syllable affiliation and voicing contrasts, two English learner groups of Korean speakers were compared with English monolinguals, and these English learners shifted their identification of the English voiced stops in "eeb" more toward [p] when the syllable was repeated at fast rates. In contrast, English monolinguals accurately identified the voiced stops as [b] all across the rate continuum. Given this finding, it is speculated that the Korean speakers' shift toward [p] is possibly due to the effect of coda neutralization in Korean where three distinct voicelss stops are allowed in syllable onset position while their three-way distinctions must be neutralized into voiceless lax stops in the syllable coda position. Thus, this coda neutralization phenomenon in Korean may bias the Korean-speaking learners of English more toward [p] when they hear the repeated stimili of English stops in the experiment. Therefore, Chapter 6 aims to further understand this possible effect of coda neutralization on the perception of English voiceless/voiced stops by Korean learners of English. It also examines the relationship between phonology and orthography regarding voicing contrasts in relation to syllable position (i.e., syllable onset vs. syllable coda positions). This is relevant because there are syllable positional asymmetries in phonology and orthography in terms of representing phonemic contrasts in Korean. That is, *syllable-initially*,three-way phonemic contrasts in Korean stops are reflected in both phonology and orthography. *Syllable-finally*, however, the phonemic contrasts undergo neutralization in Korean phonology while the orthography does not change. There are two kinds of asymmetries involved here in relation to syllable position. First, syllable initial position preserves phonemic contrasts while syllable final position neutralizes the contrasts in Korean phonology. Second, the syllable-final neutralization is captured only in the phonology, not in the orthography. These two asymmetries are schematized in Figure 6.1.

Figure 6.1. Syllable positional asymmetries in Korean

contrasts	syllable-initial	syllable-final
phonology	YES	NO Due to coda neutralization
orthography	YES	YES

In contrast, phonemic voicing contrasts in English are not syllable position-sensitive, and they are captured and represented in both phonology and orthography as shown in Table 6.1.

Table 6.1. English voicing contrasts in phonology and orthography

contrasts	syllable-initial	syllable-final
phonology	YES /p/ vs. /b/	YES /p/ vs. /b/
orthography	YES pin vs. bin	YES mop vs. mob

Possible complications, then, may arise when Korean-speaking learners of English attempt to perceive the voicing contrasts of English stops in different syllable positions. Along this line, the current chapter examines the interplay between phonology and orthography in perception of voicing contrasts of L2 English stops by Korean learners of English with a possible effect of coda neutralization from their L1 Korean. I begin this endeavor by introducing coda neutralization in Korean in the following section.

Coda Neutralization in Korean

It is well known that Korean has a three-way contrast in stops *syllable-initially*– e.g., lax stops /p, t, k/, tense stops /p', t', k'/, and aspirated stops /p^h, t^h, k^h/ - as shown in (1).

(1) Three-way distinctions of syllable initial stops in Korean

a. /p/-series

불 /**p**ul/	[**p**ul]	'fire'
뿔 /**p'**ul/	[**p'**ul]	'horn'
풀 /$\mathbf{p^h}$ul/	[$\mathbf{p^h}$ul]	'grass'

b. /t/-series

담 /**t**am/	[**t**am]	'fence'
땀 /**t'**am/	[**t'**am]	'sweat'
탐 /$\mathbf{t^h}$am/	[$\mathbf{t^h}$am]	'greed'

c. /k/-series

굴 /**k**ul/	[**k**ul]	'oyster'
꿀 /**k'**ul/	[**k'**ul]	'honey'
쿨 /$\mathbf{k^h}$ul/	[$\mathbf{k^h}$ul]	'Zzz—' the sound of breathing while sleeping

However, the three-way contrasts of syllalbe onset stops are neutralized into lax sops in the *syllable final* (or coda) position (Martin, 1951; Lee, 1972, Kim-Renaud, 1974; C.W. Kim, 1979; Chung, 1980). More specifically, there are three types of coda neutralization in Korean: 1) laryngeal, 2) manner of articulation, and 3) palatal neutralizations as shown below.[49]

49 Most examples are from Kim and Jongman (1996).

(2) Korean laryngeal neutralization in coda position

잎 /i**ph**/ [i**p**] 'leaf'
입 /i**p**/ [i**p**] 'mouth'
밑 /mi**th**/ [mi**t**] 'bottom'
믿 /mi**t**/ [mi**t**] 'to believe'
밖 /pa**k'**/ [pa**k**] 'outside'
박 /pa**k**/ [pa**k**] 'gourd'
(The squre brackets indicate pronunciations on the surface.)

(3) Neutralization of Korean manner of articulation in coda position

깃 /ki**s**/ [ki**t**] 'feather'
있 /i**s'**/ [i**t**] 'to be located'
좋 /co**h**/ [co**t**] 'to like'

(4) Korean palatal neutralization in coda position

낮 /na**c**/ [na**t**] 'daytime'
낯 /na**ch**/ [na**t**] 'face'

First, as seen in (2), all laryngeal contrasts neutralize into their homorganic voiceless lax stops. Second, (3) shows examples of fricatives /s,[50] s', h/ merging into the coronal lax stops [t] by way of manner neutralization. Finally, Korean palatals /c, c', ch/ are neutralized into a

50 The fricative /s/ can be considered either lax or aspirated:

a) Phonologically, the /s/ undergoes a post-obstruent tensing as lax stops usually do as shown below.

/pak+ta/	→ [pakt'a]	'hammer (a nail)'
/tok+ki/	→ [tokk'i]	'poison'
/pak+sa/	→ [paks'a]	'doctor'

b) However, phonetically, Korean /s/ is produced with aspiration, and it does not undergo intervocalic voicing as aspirated stops do.

/pam/	→ [pam]	'night'
/i+pam/	→ [ibam]	'this night'
/san/	→ [san]	'mountain'
/i+san/	→ [isan] *[izan]	'this mountain'
/isa/	→ [isa] *[iza]	'movement'
/t^hal/	→ [t^hal]	'mask'
/i+t^hal/	→ [it^hal]	'this mask'

lax stop [t] in the coda position as shown in (4).

Positional Asymmetries in Korean Consonants[51]

Due to the constraints on syllable structure[52] and coda neutralization, only seven sounds [p, t, k, m, n, ŋ, l] are allowed syllable finally on the surface phonetic level in Korean. Table 6.2 shows these restricted distributions of Korean consonants in terms of syllable position.

Tense stops [p', t', k'] or aspirated stops [p^h, t^h, k^h] are only allowed in syllable initial position but not in syllable final position due to coda neutralization. On the other hand, lax stops [p, t, k] are allowed either syllable initially or finally, and they may become voiced stops [b, d, g] intervocalically (or between sonorants). Interestingly, these allophonic variations between [p, t, k] and [b, d, g][53] are not reflected in Korean orthography as indicated in the table below. The mismatch between phonology and orthography is discussed in detail in terms of Korean orthographic representations for English voicing contrasts in the following section.

---

51 Korean Consonantal Phoneme Inventory (revised from Cho, 1990)

	labial	alveolar	palatal	velar	glottal
lax stop tense stop aspirated stop	p p' p^h	t t' t^h	c c' c^h	k k' k^h	
plain/aspirated fricative tense fricative		s s'			h
nasal	m	n		ŋ	
liquid		l			

52 For detailed descriptions of Korean syllable structure, see Chapter 1.

53 In English, the differences between stops /p,t,k/ and /b,d,g/ are phonemic (i.e., voiceless vs. voiced) and these stops are allowed syllable-initially, syllable-finally, and intervocalically. In contrast, the voiced forms [b,d,g] in Korean are allowed only intervocalically (e.g., between vowels, and/or between sonorants) as the allophones of lax stops /p, t, k/.

Table 6.2. Positional asymmetry in Korean consonants (adapted from Ahn 1998)

orthography	sound	syllable-initial	syllable-final	intervocalic
‘ㅂ’	[p]	Yes	Yes	No
‘ㅃ’	[p’]	Yes	No	Yes
‘ㅍ’	[p^h]	Yes	No	Yes
‘ㅂ’?	[b]	No	No	Yes
‘ㅁ’	[m]	Yes	Yes	Yes
‘ㄷ’	[t]	Yes	Yes	No
‘ㄸ’	[t’]	Yes	No	Yes
‘ㅌ’	[t^h]	Yes	No	Yes
‘ㄷ’?	[d]	No	No	Yes
‘ㅅ’	[s]	Yes	No	Yes
‘ㅆ’	[s’]	Yes	No	Yes
‘ㄹ’	[l]	No	Yes	No
‘ㄹ’	[r]	Yes	No	Yes
‘ㄴ’	[n]	Yes	Yes	Yes
‘ㅈ’	[c]	Yes	No	Yes
‘ㅉ’	[c’]	Yes	No	Yes
‘ㅊ’	[c^h]	Yes	No	Yes
‘ㄱ’	[k]	Yes	Yes	No
‘ㄲ’	[k’]	Yes	No	Yes
‘ㅋ’	[k^h]	Yes	No	Yes
‘ㄱ’?	[g]	No	No	Yes
‘ㅇ’[54]	[ŋ]	No	Yes	Yes
‘ㅎ’	[h]	Yes	No	Yes

Korean Orthography for English Voicing Contrast

Korean orthography is characterized as an alphabetic combination of consonants and vowels into a virtual syllabic block with a relatively transparent one-to-one mapping between letters and sounds as shown in (5).

54 The symbol ‘ㅇ’ in Korean orthography ‘앙’ [ahŋ] has two different sound values depending on syllable position: 1) syllable initially, it has no sound value [∅] functioning just as a filler for onset position while it has the sound value of velar nasal [ŋ] syllable-finally.

(5) Korean orthographic representations

a. '한기' [hanki] "coldness"

letter	ㅎ	ㅏ	ㄴ	ㄱ	ㅣ
	|	|	|	|	|
sound	[h]	[a]	[n]	[k]	[i]
	|	|	|	|	|
	C	V	C	C	V

syllable 한-기 han-ki (2 syllables)

b. '학기' [hakki] "semester"

letter	ㅎ	ㅏ	ㄱ	ㄱ	ㅣ
	|	|	|	|	|
sound	[h]	[a]	[k]	[k]	[i]
	|	|	|	|	|
	C	V	C	C	V

syllable 학-기 hak-ki (2 syllables)

(C: consonant; V: vowel)

As shown, the same letter corresponds to the same sound, and each syllable consists of a combination of consonants and vowels. Letters – e.g., '한[han]', '기[ki]', '학[hak]', '기[ki]'- are arranged into syllabic units, and thus Korean orthography inherently shows clear syllable divisions within words.

Now, I turn to the ways in which Korean orthography represents voicing contrasts of English stops. As shown in the phoneme inventory in Footnote 51 in this chapter, Korean has no categorized phonemic distinctions between voiced and voiceless stops. As also mentioned earlier, Korean has syllable positional asymmetries in terms of the distribution of phonemic contrasts in phonology and its mismatched representations of the contrasts in orthography as shown in Table 6.3.

Table 6.3. Syllable positional asymmetries in Korean

onset			**coda**		
grapheme (orthography)	phoneme (phonology)	surface form	grapheme (orthography)	phoneme (phonology)	surface from
ㅂ	/p/	→ [p]	ㅂ	/p/	↘
ㅃ	/p'/	→ [p']	N/A	N/A	**[p]**
ㅍ	/pʰ/	→ [pʰ]	ㅍ	/pʰ/	↗

Given this, a question may arise: How does Korean orthography represent voicing contrasts of English stops in coda positions? In principle, there is a one-to-one orthographic substitution tendency between English and Korean orthographies: A tendency to substitute Korean ‘ㅍ, ㅌ, ㅋ /p^h, t^h, k^h/’ for English voiceless stops /p, t, k/, and Korean ‘ㅂ, ㄷ, ㄱ /p, t, k/’ for English voiced stops /b, d, g/ as shown in Table 6.4.

Table 6.4. One-to-one substitution between English and Korean orthographies

voiceless		voiced	
English	Korean	English	Korean
p	ㅍ	b	ㅂ
t	ㅌ	d	ㄷ
k	ㅋ	g	ㄱ

Problems

However, this seemingly corresponding one-to-one orthographic substitution between English and Korean can actually be expressed by a variety of Korean orthographic representations of the English voiced/voiceless stops in coda positions as shown in (6). For example, this variety of orthographic representations for the same English stops can be seen through examining commercial products in Korean. Specifically, (6) shows commercial images captured from the Internet for products such as “Uni Wrap” (6a), “Clean-Sense Wrap” (6b), popcorn (6c & 6d), “Bob the builder” (6e) and “Too Old to Hip Hop” (6f).

My interest lies in the ways in which the Korean orthographic forms represent the voiced or voiceless English stops in coda position in (6). Interestingly, the same English word “wrap” was represented with two variations of Korean orthography. That is, as shown in (6a) and (6b), the syllable final /p/ in “wrap” was represented with the two different Korean graphemes /ㅂ/ and /ㅍ/ as in either “랩” (i.e., p-to-ㅂ) or “랲” (i.e., p-to-ㅍ). This is also shown with the transliteration of the word “popcorn”: Either as “팝콘” (p-to-ㅂ) or “팦콘” (p-to-ㅍ) as shown in (6c) and (6d).

(6) Korean orthographic variants for English voicelss/voiced stops in syllable coda position[55]

a. Wra**p**→ 랩

b. Wra**p**→ 랲

c. Po**p**corn →팝콘

d. Po**p**corn →팦콘

e. Bo**b** the builder →밥

f. Hi**p** ho**p**→ 힙합

55 Images are captured from the Internet.

On the other hand, the syllable final stops /b/ and /p/ in "Bob" and "Hip Hop" are represented with the same identical grapheme / ㅂ / "밥" and "힙 합"as in (6e) and (6f), each.

It is therefore clear that there are challenges to representing voicing contrasts of English stops in coda positions with Korean orthogrphy as summarized in Table 6.5.

Table 6.5. Challenges of Korean orthography for voicing contrasts in English

voicing contrasts of English stops in coda position	Korean orthographic representation of the contrasts
wra**p**	· 랩/p-to- ㅂ /or · 랲 /p-to- ㅍ /
Bo**b**	밥 /b-to- ㅂ /
Hi**p**	힙 /p-to- ㅂ /

In the next section, I closely examine these challenges by hypothesizing three different positions.

Hypotheses

As shown in Table 6.4 above,voicing contrasts of English stops in syllable onset position can be differentiated with Korean orthography in a one-to-one corresponding manner (i.e., p-to- ㅍ; b-to- ㅂ). When it comes to syllable coda position, however, the voiced/voicelss distinctions of English stops seem to be neutralized in Korean orthography as both /b/ and /p/ in the coda position are represented with the same Korean orthographic representation ' ㅂ 'as in (6e) and (6f). What makes things more complicated is that, *sometimes*, English voiced/voiceless stops in the coda position seem to be differentiated in Korean orthographic representations in the one-to-one corresponding manner as in (6a) through (6d).

Given this, one possible position is that it is possibly due to the coda neutralization phenomenon in Korean. As mentioned, there is no voicing contrast in Korean phonology, and yet, if a situation arises to require representing in L1 orthography voicing contrasts from loanwords (such as from English), then, one possibility will be that the orthography tends to rely on phonology from the native language for representing these non-native contrasts. That is, as the three-way distinction of stops are neutralized into one voiceless lax stop for Korean words, it may also affect the ways in which its orthography represents non-native contrasts for loanwords (i.e., it also neutralizes orthographic represenation in the coda position).If this is the case, due to the coda neutralization phenomenon in Korean phonology, syllable final stops in 'Bo<u>b</u>' and 'bo<u>p</u>' may be indistinguishable to the ears of Korean-speaking learners of English. Thus, if this coda neutralization in Korean plays a role in the perception of voicing contrasts in English, the orthography will reflect this coda neutralization, and thus, resulting in the neutralized orthographic form 'ㅂ' in coda position:

- Hypothesis 1: English voicing contrasts in syllable coda position (e.g., 'po<u>p</u>' vs. 'po<u>b</u>') are perceptively neutralized due to the effect of coda neutralization in Korean. The neutralized /p/ and /b/ in coda position, then, will tend to be perceived as voiceless [p] just as the three-way stops are neutralized into a voiceless lax stop in Korean. Reflecting this coda neutralization effect, Korean orthography for English /p/ and /b/ is also neutralized into 'ㅂ'in the coda position.This will further bias native speakers of Korean toward [p].

Alternatively, given the one-to-one correspondence tendency of 'ㅍ' for voiceless stops /p/ and 'ㅂ' for voiced stops /b/ in syllable onset position, it is possible that Korean orthography simply reflects a neutralization phenomenon into simplification, but it may not necessarily indicate the nature of the neutralization. That is, the three-way distinction in Korean stops is simply neutralized into one stop (i.e., lax stops) and represented as a neutralized form 'ㅂ' in the orthography as well. But the neutralized orthographic form 'ㅂ' in the coda position does not necessarily indicate a voiceless stop. Rather, as shown in Table 6.4, if the one-to-one substitution tendency between Korean and English plays a greater role, the neutralized orthographic form 'ㅂ' may rather bias the Korean listeners toward [b] in perception:

- Hypothesis 2: English voicing contrasts in the coda position (e.g., 'pop' vs. 'pob') are neutralized in perception, and also in orthography (i.e., neutralized into ㅂ). Since there is a strong tendency of one-to-one orthographic substitution between Korean and English (i.e., p-to-ㅍ; b-to-ㅂ), the neutralized form 'ㅂ' in Korean orthography will bias the Korean listeners toward [b] in perception.

Another possibility is that, to the ears of Korean learners of English, English voicing contrasts of 'pop' and 'pob' in coda position are intact (i.e., they are not neutralized at all), and thus, they will be represented differently in the Korean orthography, accordingly:

- Hypothesis 3: English voicing contrasts in syllable coda position are not neutralized in perception, and thus, their distinctions will be maintained in Korean orthography, as well.

These hypotheses can be illustrated in (7).

(7) Is 'ㅂ' in 팝(in the coda position) perceived [b] or [p]?

a. **With** the interference from coda neutralization in Korean

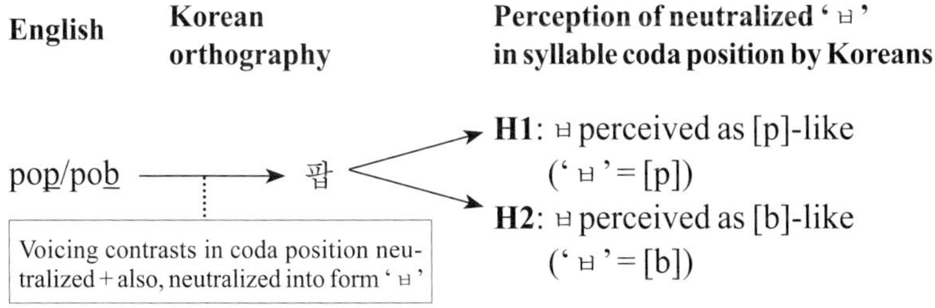

b. **Without** the interference from coda neutralization in Korean

pop ⟶ 팦 (‘ㅍ’=[p]) **H3**: No neutralization either in phonology nor orthography
pob ⟶ 팝 (‘ㅂ’=[b])

Voicing contrasts in coda position intact + thus, differentiated orthogrphfic forms ‘ㅍ’&‘ㅂ’

Methods

The current experiment was designed to investigate how Korean orthography interacts with phonology by examining Korean learners' perception of voicing contrasts of English stops in the syllable coda position. Specifically, it examines the possibility of the Korean coda neutralization effect on orthography, or *vice versa*, in perception of English voicing contrasts by utilizing two different orthography–1) English and 2) Korean – in the identification tasks.

Participants

A group of 20 Korean-speaking learners of English were assigned to sessions with English display. In comparison, another group of 20 Korean speakers were examined, this time, with Korean display to examine the group differences between the two in their identification of voicing contrasts of English stops in syllable coda positions. All the participants were recruited from the undergraduate student population at a South Korean University in Seoul, and had no self-reported speech or hearing disorders. Each participant was paid equivalent of 10 US dollars for their participation. In addition, eighteen English monolinguals participated as a control group.[56]

56 They were the same English monolinguals who participated in the experiments in Chapters 4 and 5.

Stimuli and Procedure

Stimuli for the current experiment were the same as in the experiment in Chapter 5. Since the experiment used two different displays – 1) English and 2) Korean – the oral instructions were given in the corresponding to the language. That is, when the Korean-speaking learners of English took part in the experiment with the English display condition, they were given oral instructions in English[57] while the other 20 Korean speakers were instructed in Korean alone when they did the experiment with the Korean display condition.

The two groups of participants were provided with headphones and a computer and were asked to identify what they heard after the stimuli were played. There were four possible choices. The English group's four choices: 'bee', 'pea', 'eeb', 'eep'; the Korean group was presented with those same syllables, but in Korean orthography: '비', '피', '입', '잎'. The participants would choose the best option for each stimulus by clicking a mouse on the correct syllable displayed on a computer screen as shown in (8).

(8) Task: Identify what you just heard by clicking on the computer monitor,

a. English display

eeb	pea
bee	eep

b. Korean display

잎	피
비	입

Prior to the experiment, there was a brief practice session in which eight trials were given to familiarize the participants with the task. None of them reported any difficulty with the task.

57 For a clear understanding of the nature of the experiment task, written instructions in Korean were also given to each participant before experimentation.

Results

Perception of Voicing in Coda Stops /p/ in 'eep'

Figure 6.2 shows the percentage of correct identification of voicing from the stimuli 'eep' by the two groups of Korean participants which was compared with that of an English control group. As in the experiments in Chapters 4 and 5, the speech rate increased from slow to fast and the participants' answers are tracked across the continuum of speech rate. The vertical scale (on the y-axis) shows the percentage that the Korean participants who correctly identified the stimulus as /p/ while the horizontal scale (on the x-axis) indicates the location of the stimulus in the original utterance, ranging from slow repetitions on the left to fast on the right.

Figure 6.2. Perception of voicing for the stimuli 'eep' by two groups of Korean learners and an English control group

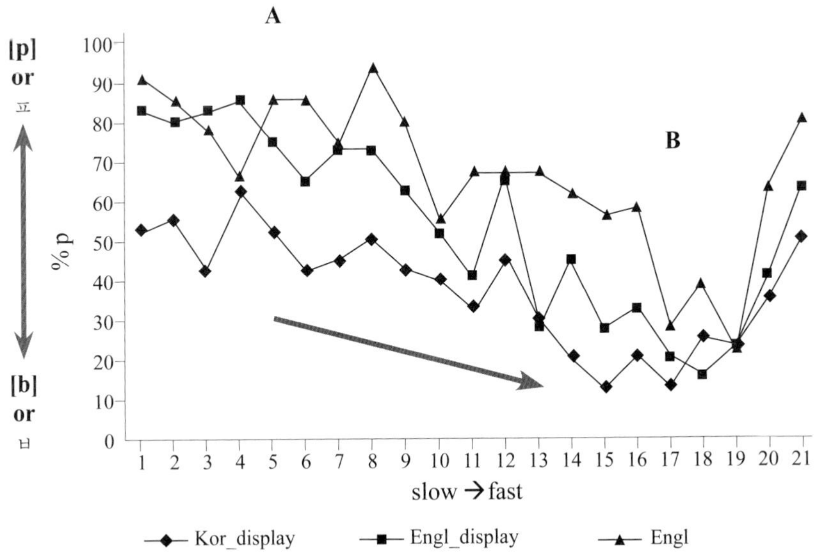

Each symbol represents a different group: 1) diamond symbols for the Korean participants who responded with the Korean language display,

2) squares for the Korean participants who responded with the English language display, and 3) triangles for the English control group (with the English language display).

Figure 6.2 shows that at slower rates (i.e., rates from 1 through 10) shown within circle A, group difference has a significant effect on the perception of voicing [$F (2, 15) = 53.856, p < .001$]. The Korean participants with the Korean display show about a chance level of identification of /p/. Whereas, the Korean group with the English display shows relatively correct identification of voicing of /p/ from 'eep' stimuli, which is also significantly different from that of the English monolingual control group. More specifically, at the slower rates, the Korean participants with the Korean display seemed to be confused in their identification of voicing of /p/ from the stimuli 'eep' with the given response choices 'ㅂ' or 'ㅍ' for /p/ (i.e., the Korean display has four choices ('비', '피', '입', and '잎') for 'eep' as shown in (8) above). This coufusion seems to result in a chance level identification of /p/ either as 'ㅂ' or 'ㅍ'. This can be translated into that the Korean participants simply chose 'ㅂ' or 'ㅍ' for /p/without confidence (e.g., responses at a chance-level).

At faster rates, as indicated by the circled area "B" (i.e., rates from 14 through 19), the two Korean groups more frequently identified [b] when hearing /p/[58] in 'eep' than the English monolingual control group did [$F (2, 6) = 31.007, p = .001$]. Furthermore, within the two Korean groups, the degree of perception toward [b] seems to be subject to the different displays. As marked in circle B, the Korean display group more frequently chose 'ㅂ' over 'ㅍ'(e.g., they chose '입' over '잎) while the Korean groups with the English display tended to chose [b] over [p] for voicing identification of 'eep' at faster rates ($p = .038$).

58 The Korean group with the Korean display showed more identification of 'ㅂ' (over 'ㅍ') for /p/.

Perception of Voicing in Coda Stops /b/ in 'eeb'

Now let us turn to identification results from the input 'eeb' in Figure 6.3. As shown, Figure 6.3 indicates that there is a consistent identification of voicing of /b/ in 'eeb' all across the listener groups. That is, all listeners, whether Koreans or English-speaking monolinguals, were relatively accurate at identifying the voicing of the coda stop /b/ in 'eeb'.

Figure 6.3. Perception of voicing for the stimuli 'eeb' by two groups of Korean learners and an English control group

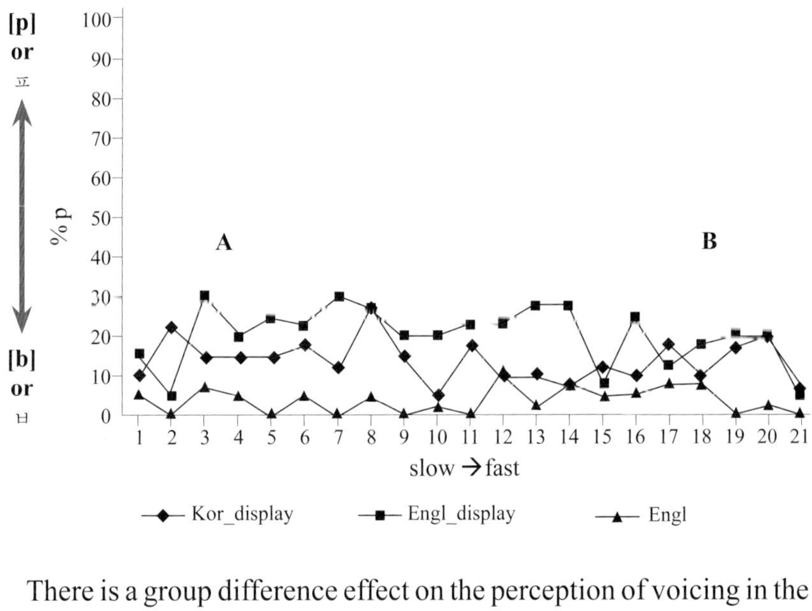

There is a group difference effect on the perception of voicing in the stimuli 'eeb': Compared with the monolingual English control group, the two Korean participant groups show a slight shift toward [p] as indicated by circles A and B [F (2, 15) = 8.323, p = .004 for "A," and F (2, 15) = 5.981, p = .012 for "B"]. There is no significant difference between the two Korean groups for either A or B. That is, there seems to be no effect of display differences in terms of voicing identification of /b/ from the stimuli 'eeb' within these two Korean groups.

Discussion

While Korean orthography is able to represent a three-way distinction of coda stops in Korean (for example, 억; 엌, 워), the phonology of neutralization in syllable coda position seems to influence people's perception of non-native contrasts. Perception of voicing contrasts of English stops can be a difficult task for Korean-speaking learners of English probably because they have no clear phonemic distinction of voicing in their own language. As reported by Major and Faudree (1996), the voiced stops in word initial position are not a big problem for Korean-speaking learners of English but many Korean learners did not perceive the vowel durational difference before voiced/voicess stops (e.g., bo**b** vs. bo**p**): A vowel is longer before a voiced consonant than before a voiceless consonant.[59] This could be related to the much poorer results in the production of word-final voiced stops by Korean learners of English in Major and Faudree's (1996) production experiment. This could also relate to the results of the identification of syllable final voiced/voiccss stops examined in this chapter.

Syllable positions seem to play a role in perception of voicing contrasts regardless of whether its voicing contrasts are phonemic or not in Korean because the perception of English voicing contrasts in onset position is relatively easier for Korean-speaking learners of English than that of voicing contrasts in coda positions. Generally speaking, orthography is a good reflex of phonology in Korean. That is, the Korean language is faithful to the principle that 'orthography represents speech as it is pronounced.'Given the undifferentiated (or neutralized) orthographic representation '밥' for both 'bop' and 'bob,'the current

59 Vowel length distinction (i.e. long vs. short vowels) is no longer contrastive in contemporary Korean. Therefore, especially younger speakers of the Standard Korean cannot tell 눈[nu:n] 'snow' (with a long vowel) from 눈 [nun] 'eye' (with a short vowel) without having contextual clues:

"눈이 예쁘다" [NUN-i ye.p'ɨ.ta. (. : syllable boundary)
a) with a long vowel [nu:n] → "The snow is beautiful."
b) with a short vowel [nun] → "Your eyes are beautiful."

chapter shows that L2 English voicing contrasts in coda position seem to be neutralized not just perceptually but also orthographically, which is impacted by coda neutralization from the L1 Korean.

Regarding the possibility of the effect of L1 orthography on L2 perception, however, the current results show mixed results. A comparison of display differences (i.e., using Korean vs. English displays) shows that biases toward [b] from stimuli 'eep'when tested with the Korean display probably come from the one-to-one orthographic correspondence between Korean and English (i.e., ' ㅍ ' for /p/; ' ㅂ ' for /b/). This supports Hypothesis 2.

As seen in Figure 6.2, however, the Korean learner group with the Korean display was not consistent in their identification of stops /p/ in coda position from stimuli 'eep' even at slower rates, which could be due to the interference from the coda neutralization in Korean. Or, they were simply not sure how to identify the voicing of 'eep' from the given choices written in Korean (i.e., 입, 잎, 피, and 비).

On the other hand, as shown in Figure 6.3., compared to the monolinugal English control group, the two Korean groups showed a slight-tendency toward [p]-like identification of voicing /b/ from stimuili 'eeb' regardless of display differences. This may support Hypothesis 1.

Silverman (1992, p. 289) proposes two distinct levels for loanword phonology:

> The input to loanword phonology is merely a superficial non-linguistic acoustic signal. Thus as host-language speakers perceive foreign forms in accordance with their indigenous phonological system (at the Perceptive Level), they instantiate native phonological representations on the acoustic signal, fitting the superficial input into the native phonological system as closely as possible (at the Operative Level).

Through loanword adaptations, non-native contrasts from L2 (such as English voicing contrasts) are introduced into L1 phonology. L1 phonological system (e.g., Korean coda neutralization) processes these L2 contrasts by fitting them into L1 phonology. The non-native L2 contrasts are, then, represented with L1 orthography that also interacts with the L1 phonology. However, this process is not necessarily unidirectional in terms of the interaction between phonology and orthography. It could be bi-directional. Or at least the orthography may affect its phonology to some extent. These multi-layered processes can be schematized in (9).

(9) Phonology, orthography, and perception of non-native contrasts

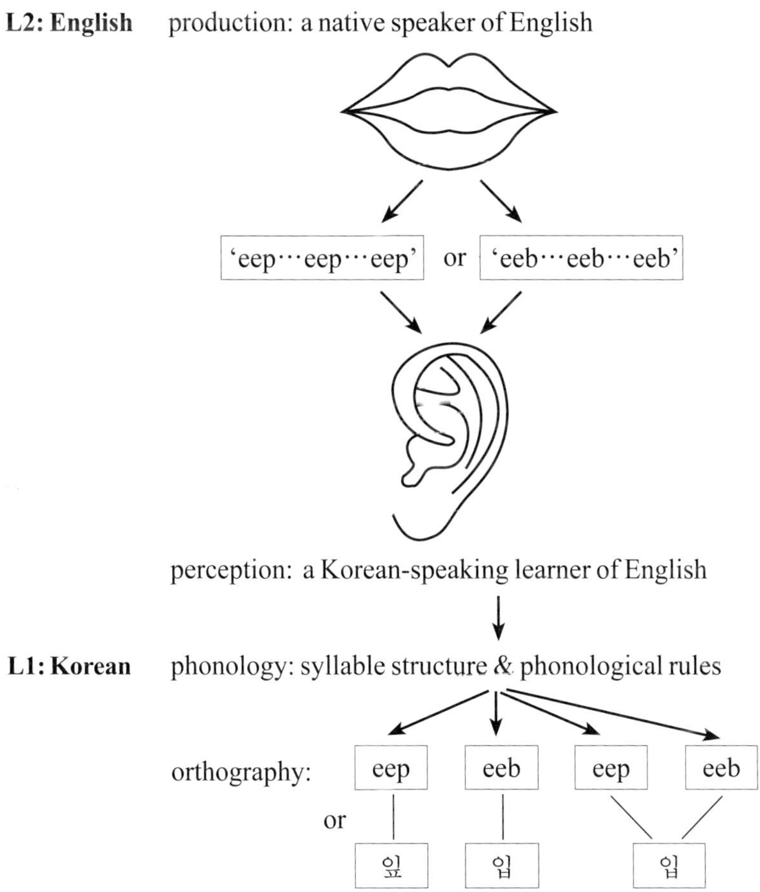

Summary

The findings from the current chapter are summarized in (10).

(10) Results from the experiment in Chapter 6

a. Perception of voicing in 'eep'

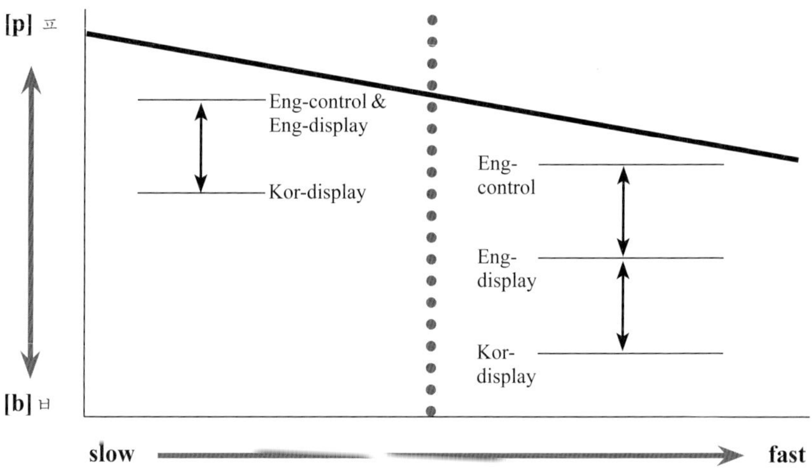

b. Perception of voicing in 'eeb'

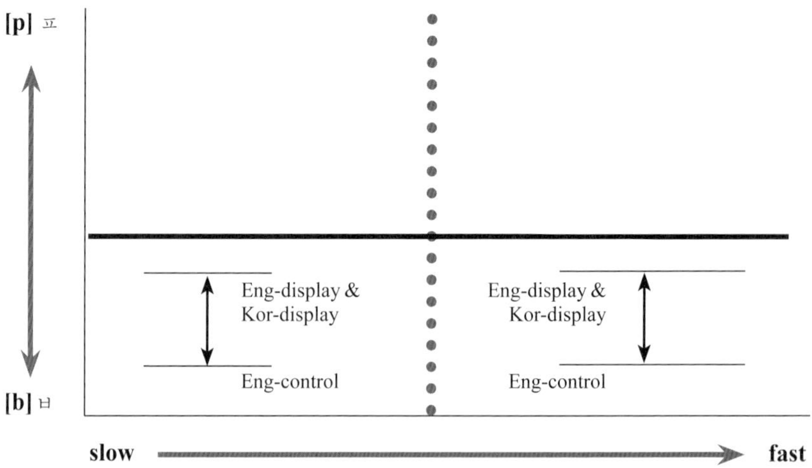

Chapter 6 explored the possibility of the coda neutralization effect from L1 on the perception of L2 contrasts. It also examined the relationship between phonology and orthography regarding voicing contrasts in relation to syllable position (i.e., syllable onset vs. syllable coda positions). The coda neutralization in Korean seems to affect the way in which Korean orthography represents English voicing contrasts. The results also show that L1 orthography has variedly affected L2 perception. As shown in (10a), the voicing identification of /p/ in 'eep' tends to be perceived as [b] as speech rate increases. The Korean display condition may cause confusion or may bias the listeners toward [b] compared with the English display condition. This is probably because the one-to-one (i.e., 'ㅂ-to-b'; 'ㅍ-to-p') substitution in orthography biases (or at least influences) the Korean-speaking learners of English more toward [b] perception when they are tested with the Korean display in contrast to when they are tested with the English display for voicing identification.

On the other hand, as shown in (10b), the voicing identification of /b/ in 'eeb' seems to be consistently accurate across the listener groups. However, both Korean learner groups, regardless of display conditions, seem to have a slight bias toward [p] compared with the monolingual English control group.

CHAPTER 7
CONCLUSION

Introduction

This book examined three issues concerning segmentation and voicing contrasts from various angles including production, perception, orthography and second language learning. First, I focused on whether and how a certain segmentation strategy observed in a language is maintained when the speaker is parsing typologically different languages. Then I examined how the segmentation process captures an intervocalic segment, and aligns it with the preceding syllable, as the syllable coda, with the onset of the following syllable, or with a joint association to both syllables, i.e., *ambisyllaic*. I was particularly interested in cross-linguistic variation in English as a second language (ESL) Korean learners' perceptions of ambisyllabic articulations of intervocalic consonants in English.

Finally, I attempted to understand how written forms of languages relate not just to pronunciation, but also to other levels of linguistic knowledge by closely examining Korean orthographic representations of English words.

In the following sections, I provide a summary of the major findings of the book, some implications for the study of segmentation in second/foreign language learning, and propose an agenda for future research.

Summary of Findings

In **Chapter 2**, it was shown that a parsing strategy — segmentation based predominantly on CV-based structure, in a native language (L1: Korean)

— was employed even in the segmentation of the target language (L2: English). In addition, other questions which emerged from the investigation were explored: "To what extent do the three significant factors in English syllabification, 1) category of intervocalic consonants, 2) stress placement, and 3) spelling, affect Korean speakers' segmentation in bisyllabic English words?" An effect of sonority of intervocalic consonants was observed in that only the liquid /l/ was treated as ambisyllabic while the other consonants were all assigned to the following syllable as an onset. More specifically, by Korean-speaking learners of English, the English intervocalic consonants were consistently assigned to the second syllable as V-CV for obstruents, nasals, and the liquid /r/ while treated as ambisyllabic for the liquid /l/, independent of the stress placement and the spelling of those consonants.

In **Chapter 3**, a typological approach was introduced to examine the relationship between segmentation and syllable counting. English speakers seem to be able to say how many syllables are contained in a word without much difficulty whereas they have somewhat more difficulty determining where each syllable starts or ends (cf. Abercrombie, 1967; Erickson et al., 1999). On the other hand, Korean speakers rarely reveal amibiguity in the syllable divisions of English words while they demonstrate inconsistency in how they count the syllables of English words. Relevant factors for English segmentation, including stress-placement, phonetic nature of word-final segment, and word-final vowel quality, were manipulated to see how these factors would affect the Korean learners' syllable counts of English words. Findings showed that Koreans' syllable counts were sensitive to word-final segments: Bisyllabic English words with word-final stops often tend to be counted as having more than two syllables while words ending with either a nasal or liquid are generally counted as bisyllabic. It was also shown that word-final diphthongs only, but not word-final tense (or long) vowels, tend to be counted as two separate vowels by Korean listeners.

Considering a hypothesis in which "rhythm is considered a central organizing factor in speech perception and production" (Erickson et al., 1999 p. 1479), the inconsistency in syllable counting of English words by Koreans reported in Chapter 3 indicates that Korean-speaking learners of English may have difficulty perceiving the basic rhythm-bearing units of English. As suggested in Erickson et al. (1999), the L1 rhythmic units (the CV-based syllable for Korean) may interfere with L2 rhythmic units (strong-syllable based for English (cf. Cutler & Norris, 1988)) in perceiving L2 words.

In **Chapters 4** and **5**, I employed a new paradigm, *a repetitive speech task*, to examine the relationship between production and perception under systematically varied conditions. Repetitive speech production was systematically controlled by using a metronome with increasing rates starting from slow (450ms/syllable) to fast rate (200ms/syllable). Perception of repetitive speech was made to probe perceptual patterns of dynamic modulation of syllable structures as a function of speech (cf. de Jong, 2001a; 2001b). By using repetitive speech with systematically controlled rates, I re-visited an observation by Stetson (1951) that singleton coda consonants (VC syllable structure) are perceived as onset consonants (CV syllable structure) as speech rate increases by testing English speakers (in Chapter 4) and Korean speakers (in Chapter 5). Results showed that Korean speakers perceived this dynamic resyllabification (from VC to CV) in a pattern similar to that of English speakers. It was also shown that in a few details the perception of resyllabification was made in a language-specific manner as well, which seems to be attributed to the characteristics of the language background and the degree of exposure to the target language (L2).

In addition, I also tested a perceptual hierarchy between prosody and segmentation by looking at perception of voicing contrasts. "Onsets tend to be identified as voiceless while codas tend to be identified as voiced" (de Jong et al. 2002, p. 35). In other words, perception of voicing contrasts seems to be dependent on prosodic structures, but not the other way around.

Finally, **Chapter 6** explored the effect of Korean coda neutralization on the perception of English voiceless/voiced stops by Korean learners of English. It also examined the relationship between phonology and orthography regarding voicing contrasts in relation to syllable position (i.e., syllable onset vs. syllable coda positions). As is well known, Korean phonemic contrasts of stops in syllable onset position are well represented in both phonology and orthography while the contrasts in syllable coda position undergo neutralization. That is, neutralization in coda position in Korean seems to affect the way its orthography represents loanwords from English where contrasts such as voicing contrasts are well observed. The results in Chapter 6 show that there seems to be L1 orthographic effects on L2 perception; it seems that the one-to-one (i.e., 'ㅂ-to-b'; 'ㅍ-to-p') substitution in orthography biases (or at least influences) the Korean listeners toward [b] perception when they were tested with the Korean orthography in contrast to when they were tested with English display for voicing identification.

Implications

Throughout the book, the importance of the CV syllable-sized unit is addressed in perception, production and orthography in the segmentation of Korean and English by Korean learners' of English. Furthermore, it is also suggested that the CV syllable structure consists of a segmentation unit in Korean, and thus, Koreans consistently make use of this CV syllable-sized unit in segmentation. Assuming that characteristic rhythm patterns in a language affect perception and segmentation, it is implied that this CV syllable unit is a rhythmic unit in Korean.

However, considering issues regarding the relationship in the syllable structures between native language and target language, and a 'universal' or 'unmarked' CV syllable structure[60] in second language acquisition (Tarone, 1972, 1984), the argument that the CV syllable-sized unit is a segmentation unit in Korean may not be convincing. Because it is difficult to sort out where this CV syllable- based syllabification strategy comes from: It could derive from either the characteristics of

60 The standard syllabification convention is that a single intervocalic consonant belongs to the same syllable as the immediately following vowel, and a syllable boundary divides sequences of two or more adjacent consonants.

the native language or it could reflect a universal tendency. Mehler et al. (1990) argue that both infants and adults make use of a perceptual unit that corresponds roughly to the syllable. In languages like Taiwan Mandarin Chinese and Taiwanese, "syllable and morpheme boundaries coincide perfectly and the syllable would be a linguistically useful unit of segmentation" (Hung, 1996, p. 109). However, in a longitudinal child language acquisition study, Hung (1996) shows that the trochaic foot functions as a segmentation unit in Taiwan Mandarin Chinese children's speech, while the syllable acts as a segmentation unit in Taiwanese children's speech. Hung argues that during language acquisition, "Children may adapt their perceptual routines so as to exploit with maximal efficiency the rhythmic properties of their native language" (p.109). The segmentation processes characteristically used by Taiwan Mandarin children and Taiwan children differ, which is developed as a part of the mastery of the native language. That is, the speech segmentation reflects the rhythmic patterns of languages.

It is worthwhile to discuss the issue of how this CV syllable- based syllabification (or the CV syllable-sized unit as a segmentation unit in Korean) would relate to the production of English by Koreans. It has been observed that Korean learners of English tend to stress every single vowel in English words creating a "staccato effect" (Trammel, 1999). For the so-called equally stressed vowel productions of English words by Korean learners, diagnosis could be that Korean learners are not fully aware of the correct stress placement of English words not to mention of the vowel quality of the words as a result of the stress placement. The Korean learners may not be familiar with native-like syllabification, either. For example, in English an open syllable gains a coda by sharing the first consonant of a following unstressed syllable i.e., it is *ambisyllabic* as the /t/ in *city.* As shown in Chapter 2, Korean learners would segment and produce the word as 'ci-ty' [ci.t^{h}i] with a clear division before the /t/. Thus, Trammell (1999, p. 316) prescribes the following for learners of English:

> For English, native-like syllabification may be one of the keys to correct stress placement (e.g., Anderson & Jones, 1974; Juffs, 1990) as well as to correct vowel quality and duration; and these in turn are related to rhythm and intonation (Taylor, 1981; Faber, 1986; Odlin, 1989).

The following figure illustrates the relationship among syllabification, segmentation, production, and orthography of the English word 'city' by Korean learners of English.

Figure 7.1. Syllabification, segmentation, production, and orthography of the English word 'city' by Korean learners of English in comparison to those of native English speakers

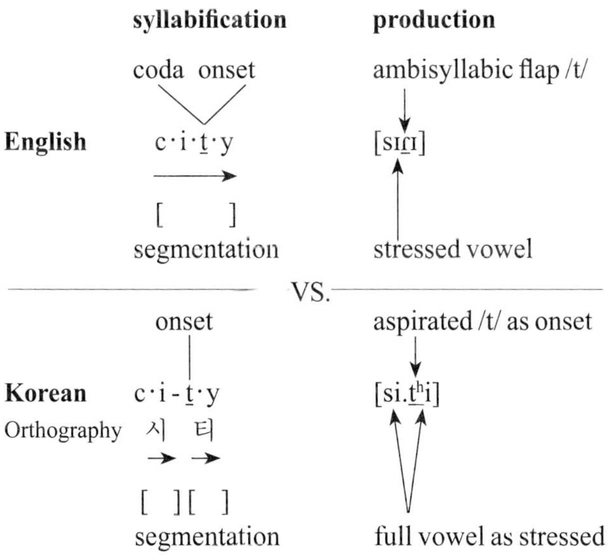

Figure 7.1. assumes that the /t/ in 'city' is syllabified as the onset of the second syllable, and thus it is produced as an aspirated stop [t^h] by Korean learners of English. The CV-syllable structure based segmentation draws a clear syllable boundary between the preceding vowel and the /t/. The segmentation process is indicated within square brackets. Since each vowel belongs to each syllabic block due to the CV-based segmentation, the vowels have the status of full vowels, which may account for

Korean learners' tendency to stress every single vowel in English words. Furthermore, the segmentation process in speech seems to be captured in the Korean orthographic representation as shown above.

Directions for Future Research

The results reported in this book have raised additional questions and suggested new areas to explore. A follow-up study is currently under way to see a better picture of the relationship between the numerous cues to voicing and the identification patterns through regression analyses of acoustic measures and perceptual responses (cf. de Jong, 2001a;2001b).

As suggested throughout the book, segmentation units may be the rhythm-bearing units (e.g., *CV-syllable based* Korean and *strong-syllable based* English). Then, to improve the L1 listeners' ability to perceive the spoken L2 language, further work is needed on the correlation between the perception of the rhythm-bearing unit of the L2 and the acquisition of the L2 (cf. Erickson et al., 1999).

Furthermore, as reported in Chapter 2, some attention should be given to the extremely low-rated Korean participants' self-rating of their English proficiency. This so-called 'humble attitude' probably reflects their cultural characteristics (cf. Lim, 2011). In Experiment 2 in Chapter 2, the original design had utilized an oral task in English. Howerver, due to the stated discomfort by the participants in doing this kind of oral task it was replaced with a written task. Gardner and Lambert (1972) propose that attitudes influence motivation, which in turn influences competence in the L2. "Motivation is defined as the effort that the learner is prepared to make in order to attain competence in L2, and his desire to achieve this goal" (Hamers & Blanc, 1989, p.235-6). Gardener (1979) demonstrated that "in bilingual environments, such as Ottawa, Montreal and Moncton, anxiety is the most important affective factor to predict learners' proficiency, whereas in unilingual environments, such as London and Ontario, motivation is the best predictor of L2 proficiency" (Hamers & Blanc, 1989, p. 238). Given the seemingly high desire to master English by Korean learners of English, the Korean participants' attitude toward English reported in this study needs further explanation.

Finally, additional research is needed on Korean orthographic variations for representing English loanwords. Table 7.1 shows some examples of Hangul Korean variants for English loanwords.

Table 7.1. Korean Hangul variants for English loanwords

English	Korean variant 1	Korean variant 2
Cake	케이크 [k^he.i. k^hɨ]	케익 [k^he.ik¬]
Yellow	옐로우 [yel.lo.u|	옐로[ycl.lo]
Juice	주스[ju.sɨ]	쥬스[jyu.sɨ]
Marx	마르크스[ma.r ɨ.k^h ɨ.s ɨ]	막스[mak.sɨ]
Clinton	클린턴[k^h ɨl.lin.t^hən]	클린톤[k^hɨl.lin.t^hon]

These Korean variants for English words basically stem from inconsistent English syllable perception, and thus, result in inconsistent syllable counts as discussed in Chapter 3. Further research on this variation in Korean orthography for English loanwords will provide ample room for applications into areas such as online Korean-English text processing and text-to-speech conversion and synthesis in Korean and English.

Conclusion

The present book focused on the decoding of continuous speech. It pursued an understanding of the information in spoken utterances and its orthographic representations and how these relate to people's mental lexicon. Cross-linguistic comparisons were emphasized since it was our main concern to understand how different components of speech comprehension processes are affected by language-specific or language universal phonological knowledge.

The current work focused mainly on whether a certain syllabification strategy observed in Korean is maintained when the Korean speaker is parsing a typologically different language, such as English. The results showed that the CV-syllable based segmentation strategy in Korean was utilized in parsing English. It was also suggested that the segmentation units (or the rhythmic units) of the native language interfere with those of target languages.

Possibly due to different segmentation units depending on target languages (L2), incomplete perception of L2 syllables by L1 listeners may lead to inconsistent syllable counts in L2 words and therefore possible inconsistent/incorrect syllable production. The results show that Korean speakers understand syllable divisions of English words in an unambiguous manner whereas their understanding of syllable counts is quite ambiguous.

Since Korean is transparent in terms of mapping sounds onto letters, it is a good testing ground for investigating how a typologically different language, whose segmentation is not clear, is perceived, parsed, and thus represented in a writing system with clear syllable divisions in words. Korean orthography is a good reflex of its phonology, which may affect perception of second languages, too.

REFERENCES

Abercrombie, D. (1967). *Elements of general phonetics*. Edinburgh: Edinburgh University Press.

Ahn, S-C. (1985). *The interplay of phonology and morphology in Korean*. Ph. D. dissertation, University of Illinois at Urbana-Champaign.

______ (1986). Syllabification process in Korean. In *Papers from the 1985 Mid American Linguistics Conference*, 1-12.

______ (1989). A revised theory of syllabic phonology. *Linguistic Journal of Korea ,13* (2), 333-362.

______ (1998). *An introduction to Korean phonology*. Seoul: Hanshin Publishing Co.

Anderson, J. M., & Jones, C. (1974). Three theses concerning phonological representations. *Journal of Linguistics, 10,* 1-26.

Appel, R., & Muysken, P. (1987). Language contact and bilingualism. London.

Aslin, R. N., Woodward, J. Z., LaMendola, N. P., & Bever, T. G. (1996). Models of word segmentation in fluent maternal speech to infants. In J. L. Morgan & and K. Demuth (Ed.), *Signal to syntax: Bootstrapping from speech to grammar in early acquisition*, 117-134. Mahwah, NJ: Lawrence Erlbaum Associate Publishers Inc.

Birch, B. M. (2002). *English L2 reading: getting to the bottom*. Mahwah, NJ: Lawrence Erlbaum Associate Publishers Inc.

Bird, S. F. (2002). *The phonetics and phonology of Lheidli intervocalic consonants*. Ph. D. dissertation, the University of Arizona.

Bloomfield, L. (1933). *Language*. New York.

Borden, G., Gerber, A. & Milsark, G. (1983). Production and perception of the /r/-/l/ contrast in Korean adults learning English. *Language Learning, 33*, 499-526.

Brent, M. R. (1999). Speech segmentation and word discovery: A computational perspective. *Trends in Cognitive Sciences, 3*(8), 294-301.

Brière, E. J., Campbell, R., & Soemarmo, M. (1968). A need for the syllable in contrastive analysis. *Journal of Verbal Learning and Verbal Behavior, 7*, 384-389.

Borowsky, T. Itô, J., & Mester, R-A. (1984). The formal representation of ambisyllabicity: Evidence from Danish. *North Eastern Linguistic Society, 14*. Amherst: GLSA.

Broselow, E. (1984). An investigation of transfer in second language phonology. *International Review of Applied Linguistics, 22*, 253-269.

Cho, Y. Y. (1990). *Parameters of consonantal assimilation*, Ph. D. dissertation, Stanford University.

Christiansen, M. H., Allen, J., & Seidenberg, M. (1998). Learning to segment speech using multiple cues. *Language Cognition Process, 13*, 221-268.

Chung, K. (1980). *Korean neutralization.* Ph. D. dissertation, University of Texas at Austin.

Chruch, K. W. (1987). Phonological parsing and lexical retrieval, *Cognition, 25*, 53-69.

Clements, G. N., & Keyser, S.J. (1983). *CV phonology*. Cambridge, MA: MIT Press.

Content, A., Kearns, R. K., & Frauenfelder, U. (2001). Boundaries versus onset in syllabic segmentation. *Journal of Memory and Language, 45*, 177-199.

Côté, M-H. & and Kharlamov, V. (2011). The impact of experimental tasks on syllabification judgments: A case study of Russian. In C. E. Cairns and Raimy, E. (Eds.). *Handbook of the Syllable,* 273-294. Brill: Leiden & Boston.

Crystal, T. H., & House, A. S. (1988). The duration of American English stop consonants: An overview. *Journal of Phonetics, 16,* 285-94.

Cutler, A., & Norris, D. (1988). The role of strong syllable in segmentation for lexical access. *Journal of Experimental Psychology: Human Perception and Performance, 14*, 113-121.

Cutler, A., Mehler, J., Norris, D., & Segui, J. (1986). The syllable's differing role in the segmentation of French and English. *Journal of Memory and Language, 25*, 385-400.

Davis, S. (1999). On the representation of initial geminates. *Phonology, 16*, 93-104.

de Jong, K. J. (2001a). Effects of syllable affiliation and consonant voicing on temporal adjustment in a repetitive speech production task. *Journal of Speech, Language, and Hearing Research, 44*, 826-840.

______ (2001b) Rate-induced resyllabification revisited. *Language and Speech, 44* (2), 197-216.

de Jong, K. J., Lim, B. J.,& Nagao, K. (2004) The perception of stop affiliation in repetitive speech. *Language and Speech, 47* (3), 241-266.

______ (2001). The perception of rate induced resyllabification in English. *The Journal of the Acoustical Society of America, 109*, p. 2311.

de Jong, K. J., Nagao, K., & Lim, B.J. (2002). The interaction of syllabification and voicing perception in American English. In T.A. Hall, B. Pompino-Marschall, & M. Rochon (Ed.), *ZAS Papers in Linguistics, 28*, 27-38.

DeKeyser, R. (2000). The robustness of critical period effects in second language acquisition. *Studies in Second Language Acquisition*, 22, 499-534.

Eckman, F. R. (1977). Markedness and the contrastive analysis hypothesis. *Language Learning, 27*, 315-330.

______ (1981a). On predicting phonological difficulty in second language acquisition. *Studies in Second Language Acquisition*, *4*, 18-30.

______ (1981b). On the naturalness of interlanguage phonological rules. *Language Learning, 31*, 195-216.

Edwards, J. (1994). *Multilingualism*. London and New York: Routledge.

Ehri, L. C., & Wilce, L. S. (1986). The influence of spellings on speech: are alveolar flaps /d/ or /t/? In D. B. Yaden & S. Templeton (Ed.), *Metalinguistic awareness and beginning literacy.* Portsmouth, NH: Heinemann.

Erickson, D. Akahane-Yamada, R., Tajima, K., & Matsumoto, K. F. (1999). Syllable counting and mora units in speech perception. In *Proceedings of the XIVth International Congress of Phonetic Sciences*, 1479-1482.

Faber, D. (1986). Teaching the rhythms of English: A new theoretical base. *International Review of Applied Linguistics, 24,* 205-216.

Flege, J. E. (1988). The production and perception of speech sounds in a foreign languages. In H. Winitz (Ed.), *Human Communication and Its Disorders, A Review 1988*, 224-401. Norwood, NJ: Ablex.

______ (1992). Speech learning in a second language. In C. Ferguson, L. Menn & C. Stoel-Gammon (Eds.), *Phonological Development: Models, Research, and Implications*, 565-604. Timonium, MD: York Press.

______ (1995). Second-language speech learning: Theory, findings, and problems. In W. Strange (Ed.), *Speech perception and linguistic experience: Issues in cross-language research,* 229-273. Timonium, MD: York Press.

______ (1999). Age of learning and second-language speech. In D. Birdsong (Ed.), *New Perspectives on the Critical Period Hypothesis for Second Language Acquisition*, 101-132. Hillsdale, NJ: Lawrence Erlbaum.

______ (2002). Interactions between the Native and Second-language Phonetic Systems. In P. Burmeister, T. Piske, & A. Rohde (Eds.), *An Integrated View of Language Development: Papers in Honor of Henning Wode*, 217-244. Trier: Wissen-schaftlicher Verlag.

______ (2003). In A. Meyer & N. Schiller (Eds.), *Phonetics and Phonology in Language Comprehension and Production, Differences and Similarities,* 319-355. Berlin: Mouton de Gruyter.

______ (2007). Language contact in bilingualism: Phonetic system interactions. In J. Cole and Hualde, J. (Eds.), *Laboratory Phonology,* 9, 353-380. Berlin: Mouton de Gruyter.

Flege, J. E., Yeni-Komshian, G. H., & Liu, S. (1999). Age constraints on second- language acquisition. *Journal of Memory and Language*, *41*, 78-104.

Flege, J. E., & Liu, S. (2001). The effects of experience on adults' acquisition of a second language. *Studies in Second Language Acquisition*, *23*, 527-552.

Gardner, R. C. (1979). Social psychological aspects of second language acquisition. In H. Giles St. R. Clair (Ed.), *Language and social psychology.* Oxford: Blackwell.

Gardner, R. C., & Lambert, W. E. (1972). *Attitudes and motivation in second language learning*. Rowley, MA: Newbury House.

Gick, B. (2003). Articulatory correlates of ambisyllabicity in English glides and liquids. In J. Local, R. Ogden & R. Temple (Eds.), *Papers in Laboratory Phonology VI: Phonetic Interpretation*, 222-236. Cambridge: Cambridge University Press.

Gim, C.-K. (1987). A study on syllable structure and phonological processes in its nucleus in Korean. *Maal* (*Speech*), *12*, 25-68. Seoul: Yonsei University Press.

Goldman, J. P., Content, A., & Frauenfelder, U. H. (1996). Comparaison des structures syllabiques en français et en anglais. Paper presented at the

21èmes Journées d'Etude sur la Parole, Avignon.

Goldsmith, J. (1976). *Autosegmental phonology*. Ph. D. dissertation, MIT, Cambridge, MA. Distributed by the Indiana University Linguistics Club, Bloomington, Indiana.

Gow, D. W., & Gordon, P. C. (1995). Lexical and prelexical influences on word segmentation: Evidence from priming. *Journal of Experimental Psychology: Human Perception and Performance,* 21, 344-359.

Grenier, G. (1984). Shifts to English as usual language by Americans of Spanish mother tongue. *Social Science Quarterly*, *62*, 537-550.

Grosjean, F. (1982). *Life with two languages*. Cambridge, MA. & London.

Haggard, M. P., Ambler, S., & Callow, M. (1970). Pitch as a voicing cue. *Journal of the Acoustical Society of America*, *47*, 613-617.

Halle, M., & Vergnaud, J. R. (1980). Three dimensional phonology. *West Coast Conference on Formal Linguistics, 1*, 207-218.

Hamers, J. F., & Blanc, M. H. (1989). *Bilinguality and bilingualism.* Cambridge: Cambridge University Press.

Han, J. I. (2002). The effect of formal instruction on acquisition of the English /r/ and /l/ by Korean speakers. *Language Research, 38* (2), 691-711.

Hayes, B. (1989). Compensatory lengthening in moraic phonology. *Linguistic Inquiry*, *20*, 253-306.

Henderson, J. B., & Repp, B. H. (1982). Is a stop consonant released when followed by another stop consonant? *Phonetica, 39*, 71-82.

Hirano, H. (1994). A constraint-based approach to Korean loanwords. *Language Research, 30* (4), 707-739.

Hohne, E.A., & Jusczyk, P. W. (1994). Two-month-old infants' sensitivity to allophonic differences. *Perception and Psychophysics*, *56*, 613-623.

Hong, Y. S. (1991). *A Sociolinguistic study of Seoul Korean.* Seoul: Seoul Computer Press.

Hooper, J. B. (1972). The syllable in phonological theory. *Language*, *48*, 525-540.

______ (1977). Syllabic and nonsyllabic issues in phonology. Preliminary version: Paper presented at the Symposium on Segment Organization and the Syllable. Boulder, Colorado.

Hume, E., Muller, J., & van Engelenhoven, A. (1997a). Non-moraic geminates in Leti. *Phonology*, *14*, 371-402.

______ (1997b). Initial geminates in Leti: Consequences for moraic theory. *Studies in the Linguistic Sciences*, *27*, 119-138.

Hung, F-S. (1996). *Prosody and the acquisition of grammatical morphemes in Chinese languages.* Bloomington, IN: Indiana University Linguistic Club Publications.

Ingram, J., & Park, S.K. (1998). Language, context, and speaker effects in the identification and discrimination of English /r/ and /l/ by Japanese and Korean listeners. *Journal of the Acoustical Society of America, 103*, 1161-1174.

Itô, J., & Mester, A. (1995). The core/periphery structure of the lexicon and constraints on reranking. In J. Beckman, S. Urbanczyk, & L. Walsh, L. (Ed.), *University of Massachusetts Occasional Papers in Linguistics 18: Papers in Optimality Theory*, 181-209.

Jakimik, J., Cole, R. A., & Rudnicky, A. I. (1985). Sound and spelling in spoken word recognition. *Journal of Memory and Language, 24*, 165-178.

Juffs, A. (1990). Tone, syllable structure and interlanguage phonology: Chinese learners' stress errors. *International Review of Applied Linguistics, 28,* 99-115.

Jun, J.-H. (1993). Prosodic approach on Korean partial reduplication. In P. Clancy (Ed.), *Japanese/Korean Linguistics* 2, 130-146. Stanford: CSLI.

______ (1994). Metrical weight consistency in Korean partial reduplication. *Phonology, 11*, 69-88.

Jusczyk, P. W. (1997). *The discovery of spoken language*. Cambridge, MA: MIT Press.

Jusczyk, P. W., Friederici, A., Wessels, J., Svenkerud, V., & Jusczyk, A. (1993). Infants' sensitivity to the sound pattern of native language words. *Journal of Memory and Language*, *32*, 402-420.

Jusczyk, P. W., Luce, P. A., & Charles-Luce, J. (1994). Infants' sensitivity to phonotactic patterns in the native language. *Journal of Memory and Language, 33*, 630-645.

Jusczyk, P. W., Hohne, E. A., & Baumann, A. (1999). Infants' sensitivity to allophonic cues for word segmentation. *Perception and Psychophysics, 61*, 1465-1476.

Kahn, D. (1976). *Syllable-based generalizations in English phonology.* Unpublished Ph. D. dissertation, MIT, Cambridge, MA. Reproduced by the Indiana University Linguistics Club, Bloomington, Indiana.

Kang, H., & Simpson, G. B. (1996). Development of semantic and phonological priming in a shallow orthography. *Developmental Psychology, 32* (5), 860-866.

Kang, H. S. (1996). English loanwords in Korean. *Studies in Phonetics, Phonology, and Morphology, 2*, 21-47.

Kang, O. M. (1996). An optimality-theoretic analysis in Korean loanword phonology. *Journal of Korean Linguistics, 28*, 113-158.

Kang, S. K. (1991). Moraic representations of ambisyllabicity: Evidence from Korean. *Studies in the Linguistic Sciences*, *21*(2), 89-100.

Kang, Y. (2003). Perceptul similarity in loanword adapation: English postvocalic word-final stops in Korean. *Phonology*, 20, 219-273.

Kim, C.-H. (1990). *Umjol Umunnon* (*The phonology of syllables*). Seoul: Hanshin Publishing Co.

Kim, C.W. (1979). Neutralization in Korean revisited. *Studies in the Linguistic Sciences*, *9*, 147-155.

Kim, C.W. & Kim, H.-Y. (1991). The character of Korean glides. *Studies in the Linguistic Sciences, 21*, 113-125.

Kim, H. S (1998). A phonetic characterization of release and non release: The case of Korean and English. *Language Research, 34*(2), 347-368

Kim, H. S., & Jongman, A. (1996). Acoustic and perceptual evidence for complete neutralization of manner of articulation in Korean. *Journal of Phonetics*, *24*, 295-312.

Kim, H.-Y. (1998). Prenucleus glides in Korean. *Studies in the Linguistic Sciences, 28*, 113-135.

Kim, J.-S., & Davis, C. (2001). Loss of rapid phonological recoding in reading Hanja, the logographic script of Korean. *Psychonomic Bulletin & Review, 8* (4), 785-790.

Kim, K.-O. & Shibatani, M. (1976). Syllabification phenomena in Korean. *Language Research, 12*, 91-98.

Kim-Renaud, Y.-K. (1974). *Korean consonantal phonology*. Ph. D. dissertation, University of Hawaii at Manoa.

Kim-Renaud, Y.-K. (Eds). (1992). *King Sejong the great: the light of fifteenth-century Korea*. Washington, D. C.: International Circle of Korean Linguistics.

Kiparsky, P. (1976). Abstractness, opacity, and global rules. In A. Koutsoudas (Ed.), *The Application and Ordering of Grammatical Rules*, 160-186. The Hague: Mouton.

Kozhevnikov, V., & Chistovich, L. (1965). *Speech: articulation and perception*. Moscow: Nauka. Translation: Joint Public Research Service, Washington D.C. JPRS 30, 543.

Ladefoged, P. (1993). *A course in phonetics.* New York: Harcourt, Brace, Jovanovich.

Lee, B.-G. (1982). A well-formedness condition in syllable structure. In I-S. Yang (Ed.), *Linguistics in the Morning Calm*. Seoul: Hanshin publishing Co.

Lee, H. (2001). English loanword phonology in Korean. *Language Research, 37* (1),177-200.

Lee, H. B. (1971). The vowel system of Seoul Korean. *Language Research, 7*(2), 19-24.

Lee, I-S., Lee, S-O, & Chae, W. (1997). *Hangukei Eoneo* (Korean Language). Seoul: Sinku Munhwasa.

Lee, K-M. (1972). *Kwukosakesul* (An introduction to the history of the Korean language). Seoul: Tower press.

Lee, P. H. (1998). Sonority-driven vowel epenthesis in L2 acquisition. *Language Research, 34*(4), 737-765.

Lee, Y. (2001). A moraic account of liquid alternation in Korean. Paper presented at the 11th Japanese/Korean linguistics conference.

Lee, Y.-S. (1994). Onset analysis of Korean on-glides. In Y.-K. Kim-Renaud (Ed.), *Theoretical Issues in Korean Linguistics*, 113-119. CSLI Publications.

Lenneberg, E. (1967). *Biological Foundations of Language.* New York: John Wiley and Sons, Inc.

Lim, B. J. (2003). *Perception, production, and orthography in syllabification in Korean and English*. Ph.D. dissertation, Indiana University.

______ (2011). Korean language education with one-on-one desktop videoconferencing, *Journal of Korean-American Education* 28: 16-21.

Lim, B. J., de Jong, K. J., & Nagao, K. (2001). Cross-language perception of syllabic affiliation: effects of voicing and language background. *The Berkeley Linguistics Society*, University of California, Berkeley, CA.

Lim, B.J., Nagao, K., & de Jong, K. J. (2003). Effects of coda neutralization and orthography on perception of voicing contrasts in English: A case study of Korean learners of English. Poster presentation at the annual meeting of Linguistic Society of American, Atlanta, GA.

Lisker, L. (1957). Closure duration and the intervocalic voiced-voiceless distinction in English. *Language, 33*, 42-49.

Lisker, L., & Abramson, A.S. (1964). A cross-language study of voicing in initial stops: acoustical measurements. *Word, 20*, 384-422.

______ (1970). The voicing dimension: Some experiments in comparative phonetics. In *Proceedings of the 6th International Congress of Phonetic Sciences.* Prague: Academia Publishing House of Czechoslavak Academy of Sciences.

Long, M. H. (1990). Maturational constraints on language development. *Studies in Second Language Acquisition, 12*(3), 251-285.

Lovins, J. B. (1975). *Loanwords and the phonological structure of Japanese.* Bloomington, IN: Indiana University Linguistics Club.

Macnamara, J. (1967). The bilingual's linguistic performance: A psychological overview. *Journal of Social Issues, 23*, 59-77.

Major, R. C., & Faudree, M. C. (1996). Markedness universals and the acquisition of voicing contrasts by Korean speakers of English. *Studies in Second Language Acquisition, 18*, 69-90.

Martin, S. (1951). Korean phonemics. *Language, 27*, 519-533.

Massaro, D., & Oden, G. (1980). Evaluation and integration of acoustic features in speech perception. *Journal of the Acoustical Society of America, 67*, 996-1013.

Mattys, S.L., & Jusczyk, P. W. (2001). Phonotactic cues for segmentation of fluent speech by infants. *Cognition, 78*, 91-121.

Mattys, S. L., Jusczyk, P. W., Luce, P. A. & Morgan, J. L. (1999). Phonotactic and prosodic effects on word segmentation in infants. *Cognitive Psychology, 38*, 465-494.

Mehler, J., Dommergues, J. Y., Frauenfelder, U., & Segui, J. (1981). The syllable's role in speech segmentation. *Journal of Verbal Learning and Verbal Behavior, 20*, 298-305.

Mehler, J., Dupoux, E., & Segui, J. (1990). Constraining models of lexical access: the onset of word recognition. In G. T. M. Altmann (Ed.), *Cognitive models of speech processing: Psycholinguistics and computational perspectives*, 236-262. Cambridge, MA: MIT Press.

Nagao, K., Lim, B. J., & de Jong, K. J. (2001). Cross-language perception of rate induced resyllabification, In *The Journal of the Acoustical Society of America, 109*, p. 2474.

Odlin, T. (1989). *Language transfer: Cross-linguistic influence in language learning*. Cambridge: Cambridge University Press.

Otake, T., Hatano, G., Cutler, A. & Mehler, J. (1993). Mora or syllable? speech segmentation in Japanese. *Journal of Memory and Language, 32*, 258-278.

Oyama, S. (1982). A sensitive period for the acquisition of a nonnative phonological system. In S. Krashen, R. Scarcella, and M. Long (Ed.), *Child-adult differences in second language acquisition*, 20-38. Rowley, MA: Newbury House.

Patkowski, M. (1989). Age and accent in a second language: A reply to James Emil Flege. *Applied Linguistics,* 11, 73-89.

Piske, T., MacKay, I. R. A., & Flege, J. E. (2001). Factors affecting degree of foreign accent in an L2: A review. *Journal of Phonetics*, *29*, 191-215.

Port, R. (1976). *The influence of speaking tempo on the duration of stressed vowel and medial stop in English trochee words*. Ph. D. dissertation, University of Connecticut.

______ (1979). The influence of tempo on stop closure duration as a cue for voicing and place. *Journal of Phonetics, 7*, 45-56.

Preston, D. R. (1993). *American Dialect Research.* Philadelphia: John Benjamins.

Preston, D. R. (1996). Whaddayaknow? The modes of folk linguistic awareness. *Language Awareness, 5*(1), 40-77.

Pulgram, E. (1970). *Syllable, Word, Nexus, Cursus.* The Hague: Mouton.

Quené, H., & Koster, M. L. (1998). Metrical segmentation in Dutch: Vowel quality of stress? *Language and Speech, 41*(2), 185-202.

Rhee, S. C., & Choi, Y, K. (2001). Yengechayongeuy moumsapipey tayhan thongkyeycek kwanchalkwa ku uyuy. [A statistical observation of vowel epenthesis in English loanwords in Korean and its significance (Written in Korean)]. *Studies in Phonetics, Phonology and Morphology, 7*(1), 153-176.

Saffran, J. R., Aslin, R. N., & Newport, E. L. (1996). Statistical learning by 8-month-old infants. *Science*, *274*, 1926-1928.

Sakow, M., & McNutt, J. C. (1993). Perception of /r/ by native speakers of

Japanese and Korean. *International Review of Applied Linguistics, 31*(1), 46-53.

Seidenberg, M. S., & Tanenhaus, M. K. (1979). Orthographic effects on rhyme monitoring. *Journal of Experimental Psychology: Human Learning and Memory*, *5*, 546-554.

Selinker, L. (1969). Language transfer. *General Linguistics, 9*, 67-92.

______ (1972). Interlanguage. *International Research in American Linguistics, 10*, 209-231.

Selkirk, E. O. (1982). The syllable. In H. Van der Hulst and N. Smith (Ed.), *The structure of phonological representation* (*Part 2)*. Dordrecht, The Netherlands: Foris.

Silverman, D. (1992). Multiple scansions in loanword phonology: Evidence from Cantonese. *Phonology*, *9*, 289-328.

Smith, J. L. (1997). Markedness and liquid alternations in Korean: Implication for the representation of ambisyllabicity. Handout from poster presentation at the Hopkins Optimality Workshop/University of Maryland Mayfest; Baltimore.

Sohn, H.-M. (1999). *The Korean Language*. Cambridge: Cambridge University Press.

Sohn, H.-S. (1987). *Underspecification in Korean Phonology.* Ph. D. dissertation, University of Illinois, Urbana-Champaign.

Soli, S. (1982). Structure and duration of vowels together specify fricative voicing. *Journal of the Acoustical Society of America, 72*, 366-378.

Steriade, D. (1993). Closure, release, and nasal contours. In M. K. Huffman and R. A. Krakow (Ed.), *Phonetics and Phonology,* 5, 401-470. Academic Press.

Stetson, R. H. (1951). *Motor Phonetics.* Amsterdam: North-Holland.

Summerfield, A. G. (1974). Towards a more detailed model for the perception of voicing contrasts. *Speech Perception, 3*, 1-26.

______ (1975). Cues, contexts and complications in the perception of voicing contrasts. *Speech Perception, 2(4)*, 99-129.

Tak, J.-Y. (1997). *Issues in Korean Consonantal Phonology*. Ph. D. dissertation, Indiana University.

Tarone, E. (1972). A suggested unit for interlingual identification in pronunciation. *TESOL Quarterly, 6*, 325-333.

______ (1976). Some influences on interlanguage phonology. *Working Papers in Bilingualism, 8*, 87-111.

______ (1984). The role of the syllable in interlanguage phonology. In Eliasson (Ed.), *Theoretical Issues in Contrastive Phonology*, 63-72. Heidelberg: Groos.

Taylor, D. S. (1981). Non-native speakers and the rhythm of English. *International Review of Applied Linguistics, 19,* 219-226.

Trammell, R. L. (1999). English ambisyllabic consonants and half-closed syllables in language teaching. *Language Learning, 49*, 311-356.

Tranel, B. (1991). CVC light syllables, geminates, and Moraic Theory. *Phonology*, *8*, 291-302.

Treiman, R., & Danis, C. (1988). Syllabification of intervocalic consonants. *Journal of Memory and Language*, *27*, 324-340.

Tuller, R., & Kelso, J. A. S. (1991). The production and perception of syllable structure. *Journal of Speech, Language, and Hearing Research*, *34*: 501-508.

Venneman, T. (1988). *Preference laws for syllable structure and the explanation of sound change.* Berlin: Mouton de Gruyter.

Vitevitch, M. S., & Luce, P. A. (1999). Probablistic phonotactics and neighborhood activation in spoken word recognition. *Journal of Memory and Language, 40*, 374-408.

Vitevitch, M. S., Luce, P. A., Pisoni, D. B., & Auer, E. T. (1999). Phonotactics, neighborhood activation, and lexical access for spoken words. *Brain and Language, 68*, 306-311.

Weinreich, U. (1953). *Languages in contact.* The Hague: Mouton.

Wells, J. C. (1982). *Accents of English 1: An introduction.* Cambridge: Cambridge University Press.

Wolfram, W., Adger, C. T., & Christian, D. (1999). *Dialects in schools and communities.* Mahwah, NJ: Lawrence Erlbaum Associate Publishers Inc.

Yeni-Komshian, G. H., Flege, J. E., & Liu, S. (2000). Pronunciation proficiency in the first and second languages of Korean-English bilinguals. *Bilingualism: Language and Cognition, 3*, 131-150.

Yoo, H. (1996). A constraint based analysis of Korean loanwords. *Studies in Phonetics, Phonology, and Morphology, 2*, 147-167.

Yopp, H. K. (1988). The validity and reliability of phonemic awareness tests.

Reading Research Quarterly, *23*, 159-177.

Zampini, M. L, & Green, K. P. (2001). The voicing contrast in English and Spanish: The relationship between perception and production. In J. L. Nicol (Ed.), *One mind, two languages: bilingual language processing*, 23-48. Massachusetts: Blackwell Publishers Inc.

APPENDIX A

1. Stimuli for Experiment 1 in Chapter 2

single C spelling, first syllable stress		
intervocalic consonant	liquid	melon, relic, relish, aloe, solace, Alex, Alice
	nasal	lemon, panic, manage, vanish, manic, Amish, tonic, ever
	obstruent	seven, epic, radish, acid, topic, logic
single C spelling, second syllable stress		
intervocalic consonant	liquid	relate, select, carouse, salon, erase, elect
	nasal	canoe, demand, deny, remorse, amuse, amaze, amount
	obstruent	depend, reveal, guitar, report, evade, adorn, obey

double C spelling, first syllable stress		
intervocalic consonant	liquid	borrow, sorrow, trolley, ballot, fellow, valley, pillow
	nasal	sonnet, Dennis, tennis, inner, bunny, penny
	obstruent	lobby, hobby, butter, fetter, baffle, buggy, Betty
double C spelling, second syllable stress		
intervocalic consonant	liquid	collide, corral, balloon, collect, arrange, array, correct
	nasal	connect, command, commit, immense, innate, announce, commend
	obstruent	support, suppose, suffice, message, attire, occur,

2. Stimuli for Experiment 2 in Chapter 2

single C spelling, first syllable stress		
intervocalic consonant	liquid	Melon, relic, lily, Julie, relic, moral, balance, pilot, color, Eric, column, serum, chili, Helen, tulip, molar, salad, iris, colic, valence, Eli
	nasal	Lemon, panic, limit, unit, venom, omen, camel, money, demon, honor, linen, rumor, moment, manage, Simon, shaman, Venus
	obstruent	Seven, epic, judo, liver, yoga, devil, vital, acid, bacon, oven, evil, profit, Yukon, vigor, motor, medal, libel, avid, baby, cover, proper, ego,
single C spelling, second syllable stress		
intervocalic consonant	liquid	Delay, salon
	nasal	Canoe, deny
	obstruent	Reveal, guitar

double C spelling, first syllable stress		
intervocalic consonant	liquid	Sorrow, valley, pillow
	nasal	Comma, penny, tennis
	obstruent	Butter, lobby, rabbit, luggage
double C spelling, second syllable stress		
intervocalic consonant	liquid	Balloon, collect, correct
	nasal	Connect, annoy, announce
	obstruent	Occur, massage

Appendix B

Representing English loanwords with Korean orthography
(By The Ministry of Education 1986, 1992; The Ministry of Education and Sports, 1995: http://www.hangul.or.kr/M4-5.htm)

1. Voiceless stops /p, t, k/

1) Word-final voiceless stops /p, t, k/ following a short vowel are represented as coda.

gap 갭 [kap¬]
cat 캣 [khat¬]
book 북 [puk¬]

2) Voiceless stops after a short vowel and before consonants other than liquids and nasals are represented as coda.

apt 앱트 [ap.t^{h}ɨ]
setback 셋백 [set.pæk¬]
act 액트 [æk.t^{h}ɨ]

3) Other than 1) and 2), word-final or pre-consonantal voiceless stops [p, t, k] are represented with an insertion of the vowel '으' 'ɨ'.

stamp 스탬프 [sɨ.t^{h}æm.p^{h}ɨ]
cape 케이프 [ke.i.p^{h}ɨ]
nest 네스트 [ne.sɨ.t^{h}ɨ]
part 파트 [p^{h}a.t^{h}ɨ]
desk 데스크 [de.sɨ.k^{h}ɨ]
make 메이크 [me.i.k^{h}ɨ]
apple 애플 [æ.p^{h}ɨl]
mattress 매트리스 [mæ.t^{h}ɨ.ɾi.sɨ]
chipmunk 치프멍크 [tʃi.p^{h}ɨ.məŋ.k^{h}ɨ]
sickness 시크니스 [ʃi.k^{h}ɨ.ni.sɨ]

2. Voiced stops /b, d, g/: word-final or pre-consonantal voiced stops are represented with an addition of the vowel '으' 'ɨ'.

bulb 벌브 [pəl.bɨ]

land 랜드 [ɾæn.dɨ]

zigzag 지그재그 [dʒi.gɨ.dʒæ.gɨ]

lobster 로브스터 [lo.bɨ.sɨ.tə]

kidnap 키드냅 [kʰi.dɨ.næp¬]

signal 시그널 [ʃi.gɨ.nəl]

3. Fricatives /s, z, f, v, θ, ð, ʃ, ʒ/

1) Word-final or pre-consonantal fricatives /s, z, f, v, θ, ð/ are represented with an inserted vowel '으' 'ɨ'.

mask 마스크 [ma.sɨ.kʰɨ]

jazz 재즈 [dʒæ.dʒɨ]

graph 그래프 [kɨ.ɾæ.pʰɨ]

olive 올리브 [ol.li.bɨ]

thrill 스릴 [sɨ.ɾil]

bathe 베이드 [be.i.dɨ]

2) Word-final /ʃ/ is represented as '시' 'ʃi', pre-consonantal /ʃ/ as '슈', 'ʃu', pre-vocalic /ʃ/ as either '샤 'ʃa', 섀 'ʃæ', 셔 'ʃə', 셰' ʃe', 쇼 'ʃo', 슈 'ʃu', or 시 'ʃi' dependent on the following vowels.

flash 플래시 [pʰɨl.læ.ʃi]

shrub 슈러브 [ʃu.ɾə.bɨ]

shark 샤크 [ʃa.kʰɨ]

shank 섕크 [ʃæŋ.kʰɨ]

fashion 패션[pʰæ.ʃən]

sheriff 셰리프 [ʃe.ɾi.pʰɨ]

shopping 쇼핑 [ʃo.pʰiŋ]

shoe 슈 [ʃu]
shim 심 [ʃim]

3) Word-final or pre-consonantal /ʒ/is represented as '지' 'dʒi' and pre-vocalic /ʒ/ as 'ㅈ' 'dʒj'

mirage 미라지 [mi.ɾa.dʒi] vision 비전 [bi.dʒjən]

4. Affricates /ts, dz, tʃ, dʒ/

1) Word-final or pre-consonantal /ts, dz/ are represented as '츠, 'tʃɨ' 즈 'dʒɨ' respectively; word-final or pre-consonantal [tʃ, dʒ] are represented as ' 치 'tʃi', 지 'dʒi'.

Keats 키츠 [kʰi.tʃɨ]
odds 오즈[o.dʒɨ]
switch 스위치 [sɨ.wi.tʃi]
bridge 브리지 [pɨ.ɾi.dʒi]
pittsburgh 피츠버그 [pʰi.tʃɨ.bə.gɨ]
hitchhike 히치하이크 [hi.tʃi.ha.i.kʰɨ]

2) Pre-vocalic /tʃ, dʒ/ are represented as ' ㅊ 'tʃ', ㅈ 'dʒ' respectively.

chart 차트 [tʃa.tʰɨ] virgin 버진 [bə.dʒin]

5. Nasals /m, n, ŋ/

1) Word-final or pre-consonantal nasals are all represented as coda.

steam 스팀 [sɨ.tʰim]
corn 콘 [kʰon]
ring 링 [ɾiŋ]
lamp 램프 [ɾæm.pʰɨ]
hint 힌트 [hin.tʰɨ]
ink 잉크 [iŋ.kʰɨ]

2) Intervocalic /ŋ/ is represented as coda to the preceding vowel.

hanging 행잉 [hæŋ.iŋ]   longing 롱잉 [ɾoŋ.iŋ]

6. Liquid [l]

1) Word-final or pre-consonantal /l/ is represented as coda

hotel 호텔 [ho.tʰel]   pulp 펄프 [pʰəl.pʰɨ]

2) Word-medially, pre-vocalic /l/ or /l/ before word-final nasals /m, n/ is represented with a doubling 'ㄹㄹ'. However, the pre-vocalic liquid /l/ before non-word final nasals /m, n/ is represented as a single 'ㄹ'

slide 슬라이드 [sɨl.la.i.dɨ]
film 필름 [pʰil.lɨm]
helm 헬름 [hel.lɨm]
swollen 스월른 [sɨ.wol.lɨn]
Hamlet 햄릿 [ham.ɾit¬]
Henry 헨리 [hen.ɾi]

7. Long vowels: the length in long vowels is not expressed in the orthography

team 팀 [tʰim]   route 루트 [ɾu.tʰi]

8. Diphthongs /ai, au, ei, oi, ou, au/: Diphthongs are represented as closer to their sound values but [ou] is represented '오', [auə] as '아워'.

time 타임 [tʰa.im]
house 하우스 [ha.u.sɨ]
skate 스케이트 [sɨ.kʰe.i.tʰɨ]
oil 오일 [o.il]
boat 보트 [bo.tʰɨ]
tower 타워 [tʰa.u.wə]

9. Glides /w, j/

1) /w/ is represented differently dependent on the following vowels.

word 워드 [wə.dɨ]
want 원트 [wən.t^hɨ]
woe 워 [wə]
wander 완더 [wan.də]
wag 왜그 [wæ.gɨ]
west 웨스트 [we.sɨ.t^hɨ]
witch 위치 [wi.tʃi]
wool 울 [wul]

2) Post-consonantal /w/is separated from the preceding consonants and belongs to the following syllable: however, /gw, hw, kw/ are tautosyllabic.

swing 스윙 [sɨ.wiŋ]
twist 트위스트 [t^hɨ.wi.sɨ.t^hɨ]
penguin 펭귄 [p^heŋ.gwin]
whistle 휘슬 [hwi.sɨl]
quarter 쿼터 [k^hwə.t^hə]

3) /y/ is combined with the following vowels resulting in complex vowels. But /ye/ after /d, l, n/ is represented as separated two vowels.

yard 야드 [ya.dɨ]
yank 얭크 [yæŋ.k^hɨ]
yearn 연 [jən]
yellow 옐로 [jel.lo]
yawn 욘 [jon]
you 유 [ju]
year 이어 [ji.ə]
Indian 인디언[in.di.ən]
battalion 버탤리언 [pə.t^hæl.li.ən]
union 유니언 [ju.ni. ən]

INDEX

T

V

Y